THE COMPLETE GIRL'S GUIDE TO CONFIDENCE

How to Feel Empowered, Build Self-Esteem, and Celebrate Your Awesomeness

Abby Swift

Copyright © 2025 Abby Swift

Published by: Bemberton Ltd

All rights reserved. No part of this book or any portion thereof may be reproduced in any form by any electronic or mechanical means without permission in writing from the publisher, except for the use of brief quotes in a book review.

The publisher accepts no legal responsibility for any action taken by the reader, including but not limited to financial losses or damages, both directly or indirectly, incurred as a result of the content in this book.

ISBN: 978-1-915833-75-4

Disclaimer: The information in this book is general and designed to be for information only. While every effort has been made to ensure it is wholly accurate and complete, it is for general information only. It is not intended, nor should it be taken as professional advice. The author gives no warranties or undertakings whatsoever concerning the content. For matters of a medical nature, the reader should consult a doctor or other healthcare professional for specific health-related advice. The reader accepts that the author is not responsible for any action, including but not limited to losses both directly or indirectly incurred by the reader as a result of the content in this book.

View all our books at **bemberton.com**

CONTENTS

5	**Introduction: Welcome to Your Power!**
11	What Is Confidence and Why Does It Matter?
21	Breaking Free from Negative Self-Talk
31	Embracing Your Strengths and Quirks
41	How to Stop Comparing Yourself to Others
53	Mistakes Are Proof You're Learning!
65	Expressing Yourself with Confidence
77	Setting Boundaries and Learning to Say "No" Guilt-Free
91	Dealing with "Mean Girls" and Peer Pressure
103	How to Handle Criticism and Rejection Like a Boss
119	How to Go After What You Want (Even When It's Scary!)
129	Facing Fears and Pushing Past Self-Doubt
139	Turning Setbacks Into Comebacks
151	How to Be a Leader in Your Own Life
163	The Power of Lifting Up Other Girls, Not Competing with Them
171	**Conclusion: Your Confidence Journey Starts Now**
174	**Sources**

BEMBERTON
BOOKS

SOMETHING FOR YOU

Thanks for buying this book. To show our appreciation, here's a **FREE** printable copy of the "Life Skills for Tweens Workbook"

WITH OVER 80 FUN ACTIVITIES **JUST FOR TWEENS!**

Scan the code to download your FREE printable copy

INTRODUCTION: WELCOME TO YOUR POWER!

"I'm not going to limit myself just because people won't accept the fact that I can do something else."
~ Dolly Parton, Grammy Award winning singer, songwriter, and musician

Welcome to your journey of building and embracing your self-confidence.

You are strong. You are beautiful. You are smart. You are enough. Repeat this mantra anytime you doubt yourself — because it's true.

You picked up this book (or maybe someone who cares about you gave it to you) for one reason: **you're worth it**. You are worthy of your goals, your dreams, and your happiness — you deserve it all.

This book isn't here to teach you how to *be* enough — you already are.

It's here to help you discover and harness your inner strength, so you can believe in yourself even more.

Here's the truth: No book can give you confidence. But learning from others' stories, hearing honest advice, and picking up powerful tools can help you feel less alone, more capable, and ready to step into your girl power.

Throughout these pages, you'll find inspiring quotes and real-life stories from amazing women — past and present — who faced struggles, grew stronger, and found their voice.

Their words should help you see that you, too, have the power to shape your life, your path, and your future.

You'll also discover that self-confidence isn't about being the best, the prettiest, or the strongest — it's about knowing your worth and understanding what you bring to the world.

Believing in yourself means trusting that you're already enough — but also knowing there's always room to grow, and that growth is part of your superpower.

As you read the advice and stories in this book, you'll start to:

- **Trust yourself more**
- **Step into the role of leader in your own life**
- **Recognize the incredible value you offer the world**

You'll learn how to:

- **Boost your confidence when it dips**
- **Turn failures into opportunities**
- **Surround yourself with people who support and respect you**

And most importantly, you'll realize that while support from others is helpful, **true self-confidence comes from within**.

PART 1:

BELIEVE IN YOURSELF (THE CONFIDENCE MINDSET)

*"Confidence isn't about being the loudest person in the room —
it's about trusting yourself and knowing you are enough,
just as you are."*
~ Unknown

1

WHAT IS CONFIDENCE AND WHY DOES IT MATTER?

Confidence is your ability to believe in yourself, your skills, talent, and abilities. When was the last time you felt confident about something? It could be when you knew you aced a test you studied hard for, or when you were up to bat at your softball game. Whatever the situation was, think about why you felt confident.

Likely, your confidence came from knowing you possessed the skills or training necessary to succeed. You spent hours studying for the test and had your best friend quiz you. You spent the last six years playing softball and had an excellent batting practice before the game.

But what about a time when your confidence failed you? Maybe you forgot a word or two while singing your audition song for the school musical, or maybe it was your first day volunteering at an animal shelter, and you were overwhelmed with everything you had to learn.

In these instances, it's important to remember the skills you do have and draw on them to boost your confidence. Confidence is simply having realistic expectations about your abilities and the inner knowledge that, even when mistakes happen or you are confronted with unfamiliar scenarios, you believe you are capable.

> **DID YOU KNOW?** Smiling can instantly boost your mood! Research has proven that smiling reduces stress, lifts our mood, and boosts our immune system.[1] So, the next time you need a quick dose of confidence, try smiling at yourself in the mirror and thinking of something positive!

Confidence Myths

Many myths exist about what confidence is or where it comes from. More often than not, beliefs in these myths are what hold people back from achieving confidence! So what are these myths, and what can you do to overcome them?

7 Big Myths About Confidence

1. People are born confident

2. Only confident people succeed

3. You can't fake confidence

4. Confidence erases nerves and self-doubt

5. Criticism and feedback are bad for confidence

6. Confidence only occurs with perfection

7. Confident people are arrogant and loud

Most myths point in the same direction. These myths tell us confidence is hard to achieve, but that's not true! Confidence is an inner belief, and only *YOU* can create the level of confidence you feel.

> "Your self-worth is determined by you.
> You don't have to depend on someone telling you who you are."
> ~ **Beyonce Knowles, Grammy Award winning singer**

Now, let's debunk them. Come back to this list the next time you feel down or need to elevate your self-confidence.

People Are Born Confident

This is probably the biggest myth about confidence. Yes, we are all born with some personality traits hardwired. Some babies are more playful and talkative than others. Some toddlers seem to take more considerable risks than some of their peers, but this alone does not equate to confidence because babies and toddlers don't even know what confidence is yet!

Confidence is, however, affected by the environment someone grows up in; so if you weren't allowed to or supported in taking risks as a child, then you may have less confidence in your abilities as a teen.

But think about all the things you *CAN* do. Confidence comes from the knowledge that we possess the ability to do something. So, the next time your confidence is lacking, remind yourself of what you're capable of and remember that you often have to try something and practice before achieving it.

Only Confident People Succeed

It may feel like only confident people succeed because success tends to breed confidence. Your confidence elevates once you know you can do something, no matter how scared you were before you tried it.

But many successful people lack confidence! Adele, Katy Perry, and Rhianna have all confessed to having horrible bouts of stage fright and anxiety when performing. Some of the biggest music stars in the world, who are praised for their voices and appearances, still get nervous before going on stage.

Gymnastic gold medalist Simone Biles withdrew from an Olympic event because of anxiety she was having. Tennis stars Serena Williams and Naomi Osaka have openly discussed their anxiety and depression at times.[2]

These are just a few very successful women who occasionally lack confidence. What makes them successful is their ability to keep trying and not be too hard on themselves when their confidence begins to lag.

You Can't Fake Confidence

You've probably heard the phrase "fake it til you make it." That's because there's a level of truth behind it. When you're feeling nervous or shaky, taking a few deep breaths, smiling, and holding your posture upright can calm your nerves and give you a boost.

Often, once you begin the task you were worried about and realize it's not a disaster, your confidence will slowly increase. Whatever it is you're doing — playing a sport, performing a musical performance, taking a test, or giving a speech — give yourself a little pep talk, remind yourself you've got this, and go out and do it looking as if you've got all the confidence in the world.

Chances are you won't be the only one faking it!

Criticism and Feedback Are Bad for Confidence

Criticism doesn't usually feel nice, but constructive and thoughtful criticism or feedback is how you learn from your mistakes and improve. If your music teacher never corrected your fingering on the violin, you might not be able to play more challenging pieces now. You might not have won a tennis championship if your coach didn't correct your backswing.

While criticism doesn't always feel great in the moment, it is crucial to step back and consider what it is teaching you, especially when it is coming from someone more experienced and in a supportive and helpful way.

Confidence Only Occurs with Perfection

By now, you should realize that confidence comes from skill and belief in one's abilities, but there is no such thing as perfection. You may get 100 percent on a big test or execute your dance solo flawlessly at the recital. But no one is perfect all the time. If you had to perform the same solo every day, eventually, you'd make a mistake, and that's OK!

Remember when you see Hollywood stars, they've had makeup artists and hair stylists help them. When your favorite athlete has a fantastic game, she's spent hours working towards that goal and will continue to work. Perfection doesn't exist. Confidence comes from believing in yourself.

Confident People Are Arrogant and Loud

This is a huge misconception about confidence. In fact, the people who are the loudest and most boastful are often the *least* confident. The bravado they put forth is to cover up insecurities they have about themselves and possibly intimidate others into feeling less confident.

Arrogance is when someone behaves or speaks as if they are more important than others. A person may boast loudly about how many runs they scored in their last game in front of their teammates or opponents. Or, while in a waiting room before an audition, a person may brag endlessly about how many solos and awards they have. These actions are usually done to intimidate others in an attempt to make the speaker seem better than they are.

Confident people typically don't have to tell everyone how good and successful they are because their abilities speak for themselves.

Confidence vs. Arrogance

The final myth discussed in the previous section is that confident people are arrogant. However, as we have already pointed out, arrogance is often used as a mask when someone lacks confidence. Arrogance might be an intimidation tool or how some have learned to cope with their low self-esteem.

However, some people are very successful and confident and end up becoming arrogant. Arrogance can also stem from overconfidence; when these people fail, they lack the skills to deal with failure and become whiny or sore losers, exacerbating their arrogance.

"Confidence is a fine trait. Overconfidence isn't."
~ Laurell K. Hamilton, American author

People with true confidence tend to be kind and helpful because they feel secure in their abilities and are not easily threatened by others. They also understand that they will not succeed at every opportunity, so they can try again when failure happens!

Additionally, confident people know that failure isn't always about them but often the situation's circumstances. For example, not getting the part you wanted in the play might have more to do with the director wanting someone taller or older looking and not your talent. Or, playing a game where you didn't score a goal could be because your knee was sore or the other team's defense was playing exceptionally well, not that you are a terrible player or were playing poorly.

REMEMBER! Confidence takes time, patience, and practice. It grows within you. Only you can control how confident you feel; others are not allowed to determine that for you! When you're feeling nervous or low on confidence, try smiling and faking it until you make it, and watch your confidence grow!

BREAKING FREE FROM NEGATIVE SELF-TALK

"If you realized how powerful your thoughts are, you would never think a negative thought."
~ **Peace Pilgrim, spiritualist and peace activist**

What is Self Talk? Why Does It Matter?

Self-talk makes up your inner and sometimes spoken thoughts; it's how you speak to and think about yourself.[3] Self-talk is extremely powerful and can alter your thoughts and feelings about yourself. Sometimes, self-talk is referred to as your inner voice.

Your inner voice can pump you up before a big game or psych you out before your band solo. It all depends on how you speak to yourself and the kinds of thoughts you have.

Girls and women tend to have especially harsh inner voices. Teens often judge themselves harshly and have a negative loop of thoughts about themselves going on inside their heads. The COVID-19 pandemic that began in March 2020 has added to the pressure teens face to fit in and feel included among peers.

Social interaction is critical for teen development, and during COVID-19, many teens were on social media more than before to interact with friends. Too much time on social media can trigger you to compare yourself to others often and this adds to a negative self-image, increasing the difficulty you might be facing.[4]

As a teen, you are also going through puberty, which affects your hormones and, as a result, your self-image. The COVID pandemic, combined with increased social media use and puberty, has increased the number of teen girls dealing with negative feelings about themselves.[5] So, don't worry, you are not alone if you are having a hard time.

Unfortunately, our brains tend to have a negative bias toward things we really don't need to worry about. So, as a teen, you are likely to focus on the negative things that happen, like a critical comment on your outfit or a rude person you encountered in a shop.

It is impossible to stop all negative thoughts. However, you can try to limit the number of negative feelings you have about yourself daily and stop them before they become obsessive, harmful, and unhealthy.

DID YOU KNOW? Some negative thoughts are natural and normal; it is referred to as negativity bias. Negativity bias is an evolutionary tool that protected our ancient ancestors. Humans who paid attention to harmful and dangerous situations were more likely to survive.[6]

Flipping the Script: Turning Negative Thoughts into Positive and Powerful Ones

"It doesn't matter if you're a size two or twenty-two; you can be healthy as long as you're taking care of your body, working out, and telling yourself 'I love you' instead of taking in the negativity of beauty standards."
~ **Ashley Graham, plus-size model**

Flipping the script, reframing, and changing your thoughts are different ways of saying that you can transform negative thoughts or self-talk into something positive.

There is a lot of power in positive self-talk. When you speak kindly and positively to yourself, it:[7]

- Improves your self-esteem, stress management, and wellbeing

- Reduces symptoms of depression and anxiety

- Reduces your risk of self-harm

- Makes you feel more in control of your life
- Helps with physical aches and pain
- Helps you to achieve your goals

Teen girls tend to share many of the same negative thoughts and feelings about themselves. The table below shows examples of girls' most common negative thoughts about themselves and how you can reframe them!

Practicing Positive Self-Talk

It's easy to say that you should do something, but it is often more challenging to put it into practice. So, how do you improve how you speak to and think about yourself?

Like all other skills, developing a pattern of positive self-talk requires practice. Start by noticing your negative thoughts. Keeping a journal can help. When you catch yourself thinking something negative, try to flip it into something positive. Even the smallest changes can begin to affect how you feel.

Surround yourself with other positive people! If your friends constantly say negative things about you and others, they are not the right people for you to be around. Even if they are only negative about themselves, that negative energy can be contagious. However, positive energy is more helpful to being confident, so find others with a positive mindset.

Lastly, identify your strengths. What is it about yourself that you *do* like about yourself? Use a journal to write down your strengths and add to them as they grow. Practice daily gratitude by writing down one thing you're grateful for each day. Even on days that feel the worst, you can be grateful you had food to eat, a home to sleep in, or that the sun was shining.

It may feel silly at first, but the more you practice positive self-talk, the more natural it will become!

The Power Pose

Body language, like how you speak to and think about yourself, can affect your feelings and boost your confidence. The power pose is a style of body language that signals confidence. It shows others you are confident and makes you feel good, too![8]

The concept of the power pose is attributed to author Amy Cudder, who wrote *Presence: How to Bring Your Best Self to Your Boldest Challenges*. She has popularized the knowledge that the power pose positively influences thoughts and behavior.

You can use a power pose anytime you need a boost of confidence. Some of the best times to use it are:

- Before an interview or audition
- Before giving a speech or presentation
- Before an athletic competition
- Before a difficult or uncomfortable conversation
- As soon as you wake up and get out of bed each morning

There are five power poses you can try![9]

The Wonder Woman pose: Feet apart and hands in fists on your hips.

The Victory Pose: Raise your arms in a V above your head.

The Vanna White: One hand on your hip, the other used to gesture outward.

The Loomer: Used when sitting, lean slightly forward in your chair, often onto another chair or desk.

The Salutation: Arms up and outstretched with your face skyward.

You can enhance your power pose by including some positive self-talk! Try looking in a mirror as you strike your favorite power pose and saying something positive aloud. A simple "I've got this" or "I am capable" is a good place to start!

Self-Talk Makeover

Try this self-talk makeover whenever you need to practice framing your thoughts, you need a boost of self-confidence, or right before bed every night so you can fall asleep feeling good about who you are!

1. Stop your negative thoughts in their tracks and identify your inner critic. Who or what tells you you aren't enough in this situation? Give your inner critic a silly name to take the power away from them. How about Sad Sally, Disrespectful Danielle, or Lying Lisa?

2. Immediately challenge your inner critic by reframing the negative thoughts you're having.

3. Take a few relaxing, deep breaths in through your nose and out through your mouth, and be in the present.

4. Celebrate a recent small win to remind yourself of your strengths. For example, getting an A on a recent assignment or singing a solo in your church choir.

5. Say a positive, self-affirming mantra. Here are a few you can try or create your own!

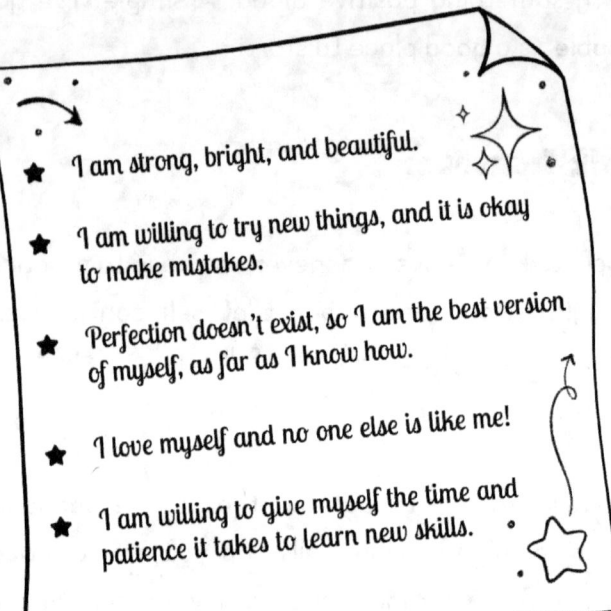

- ★ I am strong, bright, and beautiful.
- ★ I am willing to try new things, and it is okay to make mistakes.
- ★ Perfection doesn't exist, so I am the best version of myself, as far as I know how.
- ★ I love myself and no one else is like me!
- ★ I am willing to give myself the time and patience it takes to learn new skills.

REMEMBER! Self-talk is a powerful tool that you can use for good or evil! The more positively you speak to yourself, the better you'll feel about your abilities and who you are. You can't avoid all negative thoughts, but when they pop up, do your best to frame them into something positive and self-affirming. Positive self-talk is a skill and will require practice, but once you get the hang of it, you'll benefit immensely!

EMBRACING YOUR STRENGTHS AND QUIRKS

"Love yourself first, and everything else falls into line. You really have to love yourself to get anything done in this world."
*~ **Lucille Ball**, comedian and actress*

Positive self-talk is a journey to loving yourself. With enough positive self-talk, you will eventually begin to appreciate yourself more. But it's not an overnight journey. Be patient with yourself as you learn to embrace who you are, your quirks, differences, and strengths.

Confidence can only come from within. We all love compliments, praise, and other things that make us feel validated, but no matter how much external validation you receive, you must believe deep down that you deserve it.

Your confidence must come from being you, not anyone else. It is okay to look to others for support and inspiration and to help you define your goals. For example, you may look up to Michelle Kwan because you want to be a professional figure skater. Or you may admire Maya Angelou because she inspires you to write. Role models are excellent; however, you must remember that each person has their path, including you!

DID YOU KNOW? Deshauna Barber, an army captain and Miss USA 2016, lost the Miss District of Columbia Pageant five times before she made it to the Miss USA contest. But she didn't let her losses stop her. Instead, she focused on the positive and kept trying. She believes that regret should be feared more than failure because failure is an inevitable part of life, but you have to try at least to succeed!

Embracing Your Strengths

If you want to embrace your strengths, you must first discover them. You likely already know some of your strengths. You might know you're a strong swimmer or excel at writing stories. Maybe you're an award-winning gymnast or got the lead in the school musical. Some strengths are easy to identify because they are probably the things you already have confidence in and enjoy.

But what about the strengths or quirks that might be less obvious or that you don't necessarily see as a positive? In the hit musical and movie *Wicked*, the character Elphaba sings the line:

> "Did that really just happen?
> Have I actually understood?
> This weird quirk I've tried to suppress or hide
> Is a talent that can help me meet the Wizard."
> ~ **"The Wizard and I," Wicked the Musical**

She didn't see her power as something positive until she learned more about it and herself.

Identifying Your Secret Superpowers

What are your quirks that might be hidden talents? What secret superpowers are waiting to be discovered?

- Do you like to doodle? Then you're probably a creative person with an eye for shape and color.

- Are you talkative? Then you're probably friendly, social, and good at helping others.

- Do you love math and science? Then, you could tutor younger girls and inspire a love for STEM.

Identify Your Superpowers

Finding Your Quirks & Hidden Talents

What things do I enjoy doing?

What comes naturally to me?

How can I use them?

Which of them can I explore further?

Take a few minutes, and on a blank piece of paper, write down all the things you enjoy, are good at, or seem to come naturally or easily to you. What hidden strengths might these parts of you lead to? Which of them would you be interested in exploring more?

Finding and embracing your quirks does more than simply boost your confidence. Accepting who you are is key to living a happy and meaningful life.

Loving who you are and finding your hidden talents honestly does give you superpowers.

Here's How Loving Yourself Gives You Superpowers

- They help you deal with stressful people and situations.
- They help you focus on your education and learning.
- They build patience.
- They help motivate you.
- They help you control your harmful habits and impulses.
- They build inner strength and enable you to have control over your life.
- They help you make important decisions.
- They give you the courage to endure hardships and difficulties

The Stand-Out Statement

Give this exercise a try and create a personal stand-out statement. Your stand-out statement should highlight your unique strengths, skills, quirks, achievements, and anything else you're proud of!

These statements are often used on resumes and cover letters to attract the attention of potential employers or college admissions specialists. However, they can also be used to promote self-confidence and self-esteem.

Below are examples of stand-out personal statements written by high school application letters and resumes.

> *I used to be really afraid of failing. Sometimes I didn't even try things because I didn't want to mess up or feel embarrassed. But then I realized that everyone makes mistakes — and that's how we get better. Now I try to be brave, even when I feel nervous. If I fail, I know it's okay. I just think about what I learned and try again.*

> *When I feel stressed or overwhelmed, being outside always helps me feel better. I love how peaceful it is to sit in the grass, listen to birds, or just watch the clouds move. Nature is where I go when I need to feel calm, happy, or inspired. It reminds me that it's okay to slow down and just enjoy the little things.*

Ever since I picked up a camera, I've loved taking pictures. I like how a photo can make something ordinary — like a puddle or a leaf — look really cool. I'm always noticing interesting light, shadows, and colors. Photography helps me pay attention to the beauty around me, even on days when I feel blah or bored.

Music has always been a big part of my life. I love singing along to my favorite songs, making playlists, and even writing little songs of my own. Music helps me express how I feel, especially when I don't have the right words. Whether I'm happy, sad, or just need to dance around my room, music is always there for me.

Your stand-out statement doesn't need to be as wordy or detailed as these examples; these are designed as formal statements. But they give you an idea of your accomplishments and skills that you can write about. If this exercise feels overwhelming, try this. Get a blank piece of paper and pencil, answer these questions:

I Am Proud

Fill in these three statements below to craft your stand-out statement. If you have more than one achievement you're proud of or have multiple sources of pride and inspiration, write additional statements!

I am proud of myself when I

I am inspired by

My biggest achievement is

Once finished, place your statement somewhere you can see it when you need a boost of confidence. You could hang it on your bedroom wall, put a copy in your school binder, or fold it up and put it in your bag or purse.

REMEMBER! You give yourself power when you embrace your inner quirks and strengths. You should be proud of who you are and what makes you unique. Stop comparing yourself to others and rejoice that no one else is like you! And when you need a quick dose of confidence, read your stand-out statement as a reminder of why you are amazing.

HOW TO STOP COMPARING YOURSELF TO OTHERS

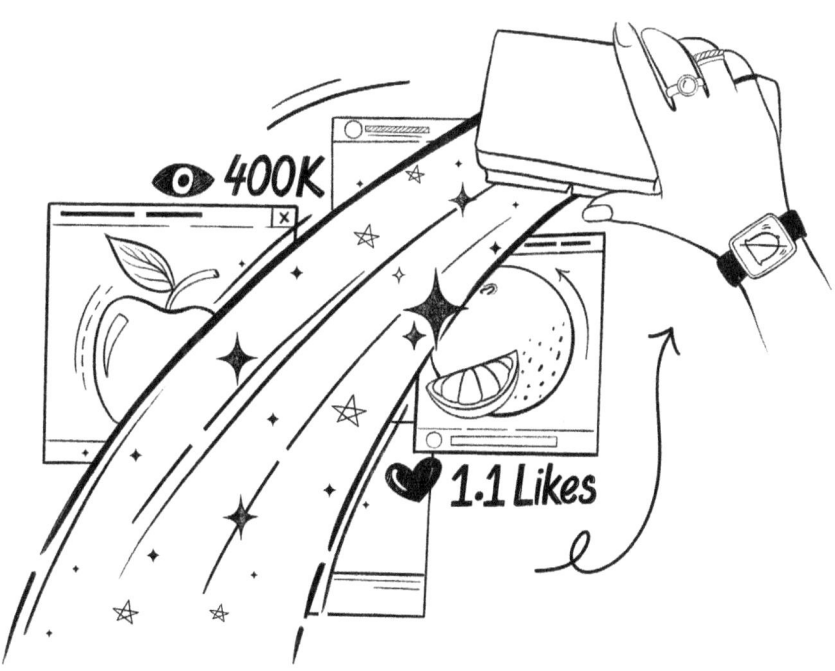

*"You have to be careful about comparing yourself to others.
You can never be somebody else.
You will only be yourself, and that's what's great."*
~ Rose Byrne, Australian actress

We all compare ourselves to others. We do it constantly, sometimes without even realizing it. We worry about what clothes to wear, how our hair looks, whether someone played better during the game, or how others performed when preparing for cheer tryouts. All day long, we compare ourselves to others.

While it is easier said than done, you should only compare yourself to yourself. Your daily goal should be to be the best version of yourself possible.

Unfortunately, social media can make it hard to stop comparing ourselves to others. Studies show that teens use social media more than any other age group, and girls spend even more time online than boys. On average, an American teenage girl spends **5.3 hours a day** on social media — that's a lot of scrolling and comparing.[10]

So, how can you stop comparing yourself to others and focus more on loving yourself?

Social Media vs. Real Life: Escape the Trap

You've probably heard it before from your parents, teachers, and other adults who care about you, but here it is one more time: **social media is not real life.** You know this is true. Think of the last selfie you took and shared with your friends; how many times did you retake it to ensure the lighting was *just* right and you liked your smile? Was it three, five, maybe even ten times?

And what about that day you had that was utterly terrible? But on social media, you posted a picture of a new pair of shoes you bought or a quote saying how beautiful the sky was.

Most of us hide the negative aspects of our lives from social media and only post the good things that make us appear happy, successful, pretty, talented, intelligent, etc.

Sometimes, people post negative content to vent frustration, seek attention, or even bully others. But overwhelmingly, social media is used to boast about life's accomplishments, big and small.

Take a few minutes right now and scroll through your socials from the past week. Take note of how many posts you put up that cast a positive light on something you did, experienced, or how you looked. How many posts did you share that stressed something negative about yourself?

Most likely, there was a big difference between the positive and negative posts. But you know, not every minute of every day is good. Maybe you failed a test or fought with your best friend. Maybe your sister borrowed your favorite skirt without asking and got ketchup on it, or your mom said you had to babysit your little brother Friday night instead of going out with your friends.

Now, remember, everyone else is doing the same. Everyone is having bad moments and bad days but not sharing them. Yes, even the celebrities and influencers. Their job is to look good. On top of looking good being their job, they have stylists, lighting specialists, and assistants to help them look good.

So, the next time you get caught in a cycle of scrolling and comparing your life to everyone else online, remember that social media is not real life.

How to Stop the Scroll and Focus on What Matters

Doomscrolling is a term coined in 2020, right around the same time people started spending more time online during the COVID-19 shutdowns. It is when you are stuck scrolling on your phone, looking at one negative thing after another. [11]

Doomscrolling is often done when you're already feeling depressed and seeking to validate your negative feelings. This habit can become dangerous because it can cause insomnia, worsen your depressive feelings, and emphasize feelings of loneliness.

For teens, doomscrolling could involve following pages of people who make you feel inferior at school or other areas of your social life, reading about experiences or events you're missing out on, or reading about news stories or current events that cause you stress.

Not all scrolling is doomscrolling, but mindless scrolling out of boredom or procrastination can be just as unhealthy. Pay attention to how scrolling makes you feel and analyze why you're doing it. Is it to avoid homework or chores, or something more positive like looking for trending ideas for a prom dress?

If you notice you feel depressed, tired, or unmotivated after scrolling sessions, below are some things you can do to help limit mindless or unhealthy social media time.

Steps to Limit Mindless and Unhealthy Social Media Time

* Move your phone to a different room while you sleep or do homework.

* Set a time limit on your phone. Most phones have a tool in the settings that, when set, will alert you once you've met your daily limit on selected sites.

* Go through your social media feeds and remove or unfollow people or feeds that make you feel negative or anxious.

* Scroll slower. Take your time to read and see what you're looking at.

* Follow people or feeds with positive posts. Try one with inspirational quotes, fashion you like, or a comedian that makes you laugh.

* Give yourself a social media break. Set a time every day or week when you don't look at social media sites for an extended time. Start with one hour a day.

* Motivate yourself to spend less time online. Set a goal and reward yourself when you reach it. For example, if you set a goal to go five days in a row not looking at any social media between 8 PM and 9 PM, make yourself a chart or mark it off somehow; once you make it five days, reward yourself with a new book you've wanted or a t-shirt from your favorite store.

Teenagers spend a lot of time on social media, and it makes sense. Connecting with friends, following trends, and keeping tabs on your favorite celebrities is fun. However, like most things, it should be used in moderation.

A 2023 study of American teenagers reported that 62 percent said they were constantly connected to Instagram and 17 percent to TikTok. Also, 71 percent said they used YouTube daily, and 47 percent reported being on Snapchat at least once a day.[12]

Reflect on your social media use. Do these numbers match the amount of time you spend on these apps? What other social media apps do you frequent? Which apps, if any, could you reduce or stop using altogether?

When you can step away from social media and focus more on the moment, appreciate personal interactions with friends and family, and spend quiet reflection time with yourself, you'll realize you don't need social media as much as you thought. Comparing yourself to others is a waste of time when you are already awesome, just as you are!

The Only Person to Compare Yourself to is Yourself

Don't waste time comparing yourself to the people you see as you scroll through your feed. Yes, some healthy competition can be motivating and positive; it can sometimes push you to reach goals like improving your tennis swing, mastering a tricky dance step, or finally getting an A on a history test.

If you need someone to compare yourself to, you can and should follow the Me vs. Yesterday Me technique. There are numerous variations of this idea, but it can be summed up by this quote by humorist and writer Jenny Lawson: "The only person you need to be better than is the person you were yesterday."

Whatever you did yesterday or the last time you attempted a specific task, focus on how you can do better this time. What steps are needed to improve? Do you need better sleep so you feel more rested? Maybe you need to add twenty minutes to your practice time each day so you can master that tricky violin fingering. Or, you might need to seek out a friend or tutor to help you prep for the next chemistry test to bring up your grade.

The "Me vs. Yesterday Me" Technique

Compare who you are today with who you were yesterday.
Fill in each section to reflect how you're growing, even in
small ways, every single day!

What I Like About Myself

My Wins

New things I want to try

One way I can grow tomorrow

ABBY SWIFT

This concept can be applied to smaller things, too. If you snapped at your little brother yesterday, apologize and focus on having more patience today. If you were five minutes late to softball practice yesterday, make a point of being early today. Make daily self-reflection[13] a habit, and you'll see your confidence and mood improve, too!

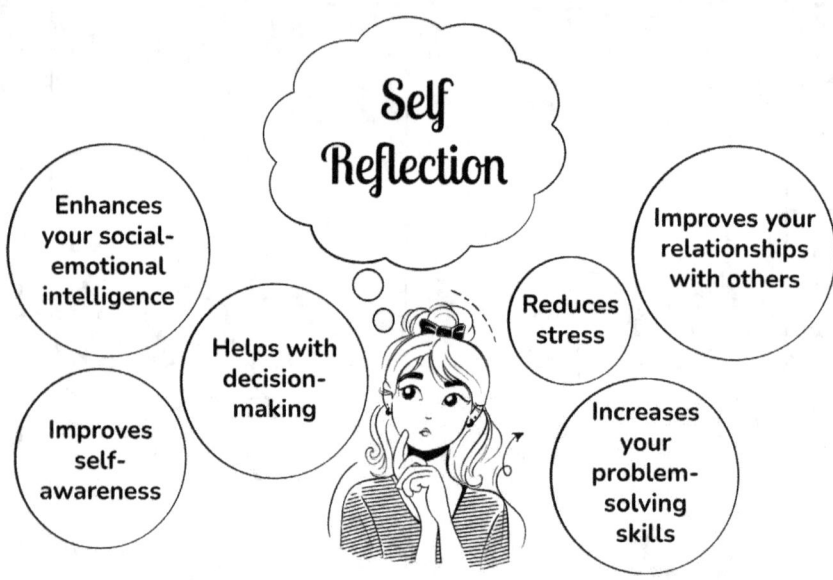

REMEMBER! A lot of what you see on social media is enhanced, staged, or downright fake, so stop using it to compare yourself to; if you catch yourself in a phase of mindless scrolling, put your phone down and do something else like listening to music or journaling. When comparing yourself to others, switch instead of comparing today's you to yesterday's or last week's you. The only person you should compete with is yourself!

5

MISTAKES ARE PROOF YOU'RE LEARNING!

"As long as you've done your best, making mistakes doesn't matter. You and I are human; we will mess up. What counts is learning from your mistakes and getting back up when life has knocked you down."
~ **Shawn Johnson, *Olympic gold medalist in gymnastics***

Erase the idea of perfection from your mind — right now.

Perfection isn't real, and it's not something anyone can actually Wachieve.

The ancient Greek philosopher Plato believed that perfection did not exist in the physical world, but only in an unseen, ideal realm. His student, the famous philosopher Aristotle, thought of perfection differently — he believed it meant reaching your full potential.

Aristotle's idea of perfection suggests that we're always striving to do better — and that's a good thing! But how would you ever really know if you've reached your full potential? The truth is, you probably won't. And that's okay.

Instead, try thinking of each new opportunity as a chance to learn, grow, and become an even better version of yourself.

Making mistakes is a natural part of being human — and it's also a big part of learning and growing. Everyone makes mistakes every single day — some big, some small. The average person makes

35,000 choices each day![14] Some are simple, like choosing Cheerios for breakfast or deciding to brush your teeth before school.

Other choices happen so quickly, you barely realize you're making them. For example, when you're texting a friend, your fingers fly across the keyboard without you stopping to think about how to spell every single word. Your brain has learned the patterns so well, it just does it automatically.

With all those choices, of course there are going to be mistakes. Think about that last text you sent — did you misspell a word or hit the wrong key? Probably. So what did you do? Maybe you slowed down a bit, or if you always misspell the same word, maybe you turned on autocorrect to help.

When you make a typing mistake, you don't call yourself stupid or get upset — you just fix it and move on. It's no big deal.

Now imagine treating your bigger mistakes the same way. What if you gave yourself that same kind of grace? What if, instead of beating yourself up, you looked at mistakes as part of learning — just like a typo? If you can do that, it becomes a whole lot easier to let go of the idea that you have to be perfect all the time.

DID YOU KNOW? Perfectionism is not a superpower; it's a fear-based response to insecurity and uncertainty. It's the opposite of a superpower because pursuing it drains your self-esteem and stalls you from action!

Perfection is a Myth: Aim for Improvement Instead

Perfection is a myth, or a better way to look at it: perfection is a trap. You can lose countless hours, days, weeks, and sometimes even years trying to attain perfection because it will never happen, no matter how hard you try.

Focusing on achieving perfection leads to frustration and often a lack of progress. You could easily lose sight of the bigger picture and fail to improve or never step out of your comfort zone for fear of making mistakes.

So why is perfection impossible?

1. It is a subjective goal. What one person deems perfect may not be ideal to another. For example, you might consider the perfect

weather 65 degrees and windy, while someone else loves 85 degrees and sunny.

2. It doesn't allow for mistakes; without them, you can't learn and grow. If you were perfect at everything the first time you tried it, life would get boring quickly!

3. Perfection isn't a stable target. Your idea of perfection will change over time. Imagine a six-year-old who drew a family portrait, and everyone in it looks like a recognizable person; to them, that may be perfection, making them feel proud. However, if they continued as an artist but at sixteen drew the same way they drew at six, they likely would not be satisfied with the results.

4. Aiming for perfection causes burnout, low self-esteem, and procrastination. It causes missed opportunities while waiting for the perfect moment.

Instead of focusing on perfection, focus on making small, achievable improvements. Small wins motivate you to keep trying and exploring. As you work towards these goals, use mistakes as a chance to learn. If something isn't working, don't focus on your mistake; focus on what needs to happen to effect change.

Have you missed your landing multiple times a week in gymnastics? Ask your coach for tips or exercises to help you solidify your landing.

Did you get a C on a test you studied hard for? Talk to your teacher about how you can improve your study habits. Is your voice cracking when trying to hit a note in a new song you're learning? Watch some singing tutorials online, or ask your vocal teacher for advice.

For every mistake, there is an actionable step you can take to start working on improvement: forget perfection.

If At First, You Don't Succeed: Famous Women Who Never Gave Up

Earlier in the book, we mentioned the army captain and beauty pageant queen Deshauna Barber, who competed five times before winning the Miss District of Columbia pageant and subsequently the title of Miss USA. But she's just one of many successful women who refused to let failures and mistakes stand in her way.

Vera Wang: Fashion designer Vera Wang began as a young Olympic hopeful in 1968. When she failed to make the US skating team, she took a position as an assistant at Vogue magazine in 1971 and, within a year, was promoted to senior fashion editor.

J.K. Rowling: The author of the Harry Potter series was rejected by twelve publishers before one agreed to publish her story about a magical boy living in a broom cupboard!

Oprah Winfrey: Billionaire and famous TV personality Oprah was fired from her first television job!

Madonna: The pop icon dropped out of college and was fired on her first day at Dunkin Donuts.

Elizabeth Arden: The founder of one of the biggest cosmetic companies first failed out of nursing school and several early jobs before taking a risk with a loan to start her own company.

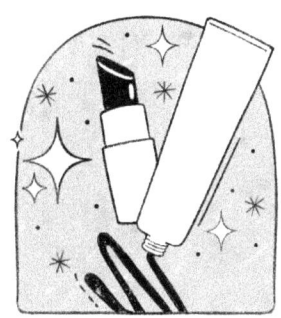

Lady Gaga: One of the world's most famous musicians, she was dropped from her first record label in 2006 after only three months.

Who are some of your role models? What do you know about their story? Read up about someone you admire and see what trials, mistakes, and failures they faced before making it big.

"Oops, I Learned" Journal

Journaling is a powerful tool for self-reflection. It reduces stress, improves mental clarity, boosts creativity, and increases self-awareness. In addition to all these benefits, journaling is private. You can write whatever you want; no one else needs to know.

A private journal is an excellent place to write about mistakes and failures and reflect on how you learned from experiences. When emotions are raw, it might be hard to reflect and learn. But if you write down your feelings, you can go back in a day, two, or a week and think about what learning opportunities exist.

"Oops, I Learned" JOURNAL

*When a mistake or failure happens that has you frustrated, write it down and come up with three things you can learn or did learn from the experience.
The more you reflect and focus on minor improvements, the closer you'll come to achieving your ultimate potential!*

What Happened?

Three Things I Learned?

How Could I do Better?

REMEMBER! It's okay to make mistakes. Making mistakes is a natural part of learning and growing. Aim for improvement over perfection when setting a goal because perfection doesn't exist. And while it might feel difficult or even frustrating, when mistakes happen, do your best to use them as learning opportunities. And who knows, failure might be the universe's way of telling you you're meant to try something different!

PART 2:

SPEAK UP AND STAND STRONG (SELF-ADVOCACY & ASSERTIVENESS)

"I learned a long time ago that the wisest thing I can do is be on my own side and be an advocate for myself and others like me."
~ Maya Angelou, poet and author

EXPRESSING YOURSELF WITH CONFIDENCE

*Self-advocacy: the action of representing oneself
or one's views or interests.*
~ Oxford Languages

The ability to speak confidently is a skill that some have naturally while others have to work at. Think back to chapter one, where we talked about confidence. Some people may be confident, while others might be faking it or overcompensating. Typically, you can speak confidently when you feel confident. That makes sense, right?

Belief in yourself and what you are saying is crucial to speaking confidently. But what if you feel confident in what you are saying but still struggle to get the words out or your point across eloquently? What if the idea of expressing yourself to others or in front of others makes you nervous even when you firmly believe what you are saying?

Well, just like learning to be more confident in who you are, your skills, talents, and uniqueness, you can also learn to express yourself with confidence!

> **DID YOU KNOW?**
>
> According to statistics, nearly 75 percent of people become nervous when speaking in front of others. Glossophobia is the fear of public speaking, and it is one of the most frequently reported fears across genders, cultures, and countries. It is experienced at the highest rates among teens and young adults.[15] Of course, some people lack confidence in much smaller, everyday situations when needing to speak up for themselves, but the fear and symptoms are similar!

When and Why to Self-Advocate

There are many situations in life where you need to self-advocate. Some are minor; McDonald's gave you a Sprite at the drive-through instead of a Coke. It might seem silly, but being able to walk back into the restaurant and ask for the correct soda is self-advocating. If getting a Sprite isn't a big deal to you, you may shrug it off and not bother, but if you've been craving that Coke all day, you'll be more motivated to speak up.

Of course, there are more significant times you might need to self-advocate, so having the confidence to do it for the small stuff will help.

When learning to speak up, assertive communication is integral to success. However, the word "assertive" occasionally gets a bad rap. We sometimes think of assertiveness and bossiness or pushiness as the same thing, especially when a female is assertive. But being assertive, when needed, is a positive action.

Asseptive Communication

Assertive communication means expressing your thoughts, ideas, and feelings respectfully and straightforwardly. When expressing yourself assertively, you should be honest, direct, and respectful of the other person.

How to Self-Advocate

When should you use assertive communication?

* Asking someone to stop a behavior
* With your teacher or boss
* With a classmate or friend who spoke or acted inappropriately
* With a friend or sibling, if there is a disagreement
* With a coach or instructor
* With a parent or guardian
* Asking for help
* Asking for advice or clarification
* Challenging a decision
* Sharing your opinion

Use "I" statements to get your point across:

* I think I deserved a better grade on this assignment. Here is why...

* I don't like when you use the word "chica" when talking to me. I don't feel comfortable when you say it because I don't know you that well.

* I think I should get a raise in my allowance because you've asked me to take on several new chores around the house since I turned 15.

* It is not OK for you to touch my shoulder when speaking to me. I feel uncomfortable when you do that.

* The record I let you borrow was returned with a scratch; I feel frustrated and can't trust you to borrow my things.

Tips to Speak Up When Needed: In Class, at Home and with Friends

> *"She had spoken it, but she trembled when it was done, conscious that her words were listened to and daring not even to try to observe their effect."*
> ~ **Jane Austen**, author, *Persuasion*

The language in the above quote is old-fashioned, yet captures the fear many teens and young women have about speaking up. Despite women's advances in the academic and professional world over the last century, many still feel their voices don't matter enough or at all. Females are also told that speaking up makes them bossy or pushy. As a result, teens and young women are sometimes fearful to speak up for themselves when needed.

But you shouldn't be. Learning to speak up for yourself is a powerful tool you can use for the remainder of your life!

You may feel different confidence levels depending on who you're speaking with. For example, if you're a strong student with higher-than-average grades, you might feel confident speaking up in class or at school. Perhaps you feel less confident at home, where you have little say in the household rules or among your friends; you might be the "quiet" one.

Or, perhaps your safe space is the school theater, where you feel comfortable among people who share your interests, and you've proven yourself to be a talented performer. However, in history class, speaking up, as yourself and not a character, to report on the War of 1812 makes you nervous.

We all have places and people where we feel more "ourselves" and more confident. So, what can you do to increase your confidence level in less comfortable situations?

Speaking Tips

- **Believe what you are saying and speak with conviction**. Make statements; don't phrase your comments as questions or possibilities. Support your statements with additional information.

  » For example, "Drake's new album is amazing. The lyrics are very powerful." You stated your opinion and why you believe it. However, if you said, "Don't you think Drake's new album is amazing? Aren't the lyrics powerful?" You are seeking someone else's opinion to validate yours.

- **Make eye contact when speaking.** In Western culture, eye contact is a sign of respect and displays confidence. You can practice by speaking to yourself in a mirror.

- **Practice ahead of time.** If you have to present to your class, speak up to your friend about the shoes she borrowed and returned stained, or you want to ask your parents to extend your curfew by one hour so you can go to a late movie Friday night, practice what you're going to say ahead of time.

    » You can practice with a friend or family member or use the mirror!

    » Try writing down your thoughts to organize them. For example:

        ▫ The issue on my mind is...

        ▫ What I think or feel about it...

        ▫ The person I need to talk to about it...

        ▫ What I believe is the solution...

- **Know your audience.** This is an integral part of speaking with confidence and getting results. Know what interests or concerns them and the best way and time to approach them.

If you're approaching a strict teacher and would like a re-do on an assignment, approach them respectfully and courteously. State the specific details you'd like to change and ask any clarifying questions you still have to show you want to learn.

If you're asking your mom for an additional $50 to purchase the new soccer shoes you want, but you know money has been tight, offer to help with additional chores around the house, babysit your sister for free for a few nights, or pay her back out of your allowance.

- **Take your time.** Nerves can make you rush when speaking. A deep breath will settle some nerves and clear your mind before you begin. Take your time, speak slowly and clearly, and avoid slang when speaking to adults or trying to convey a serious or important situation.

- **Use confident body language.** Remember the power poses from Chapter 2? Body language can convey confidence as much as the words you're using. If you look confident, you'll feel confident.

My Confidence Script

If, after reading this chapter, you still feel wobbly about speaking up in a situation or presentation, use the Confidence Script and prompts below as a template to help you prepare.

1. Do you have a few minutes to talk? I'd like to discuss _____ with you.

2. I need help with _____ Could you help me brainstorm?

3. I believe _____ Because _____

4. When _____ happens. I feel _____

5. I have a few questions about _____ Is now a good time to talk?

> I find this difficult to discuss, so can you provide me with a safe space to talk?

> I respect your opinion, but

> I appreciate the offer of help, but I can do this.

ADD YOUR OWN

REMEMBER! Being assertive means speaking up respectfully for your beliefs or feelings. Assertive communication is OK as long as it remains calm and respectful. If you need help, feel a situation is unfair, have had your feelings hurt by someone's actions or words, or just want to share your opinion, learning to speak up will benefit you. Don't be afraid of your voice and your words; let them empower you and build your confidence!

SETTING BOUNDARIES AND LEARNING TO SAY "NO" GUILT-FREE

"Boundaries define our limits and respect our peace."
~ Brené Brown, public speaker, author, and university professor

> **DID YOU KNOW?** Boundaries can upset others, especially when new. Expect this. Know that it is not your responsibility to fix others' feelings. Only you can permit yourself to create and maintain a boundary because only you know what you need to feel healthy and comfortable. Trust yourself when it comes to knowing what you need. If you need insight on a boundary you're thinking of setting, talk about it with a trusted friend or adult.

A boundary is an invisible line between yourself and someone else that protects you in some way. It typically concerns actions, words, and behaviors you will and will not accept. For example, not answering any text messages or social media posts after 11 p.m. is a boundary that protects your mental health and helps you get a good night's rest. Or you might have a boundary that you won't accept any babysitting gigs with less than twenty-four hours' notice; this protects your personal time.

You may have some boundaries that apply to everyone or some that only apply to specific people or situations. Your needs and well-being determine how many boundaries you have, when and why they are established, and with whom.

Boundaries are essentially learning how to say "no" in a respectful way.

Types of Boundaries

Most mental health professionals recognize six main categories of boundaries: emotional, time, material, intellectual, intimate, and physical.[16]

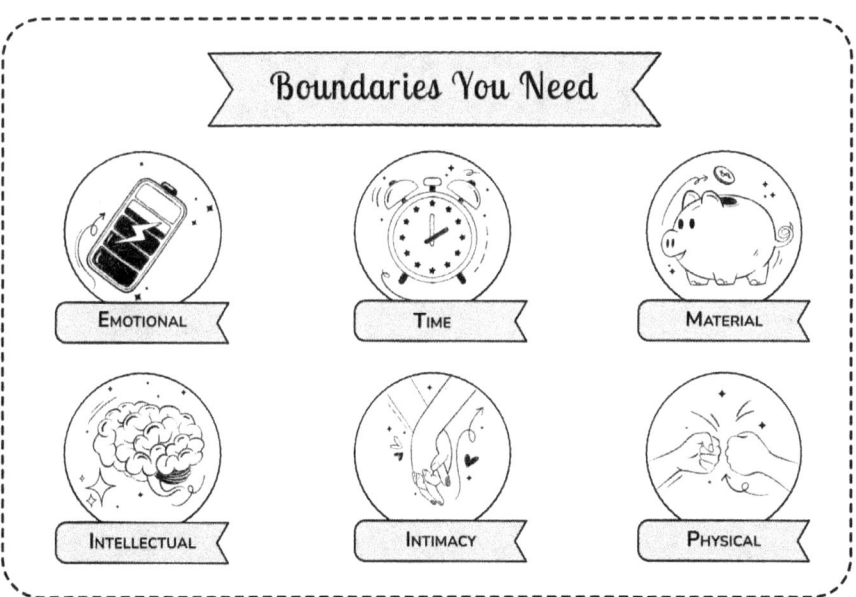

What do these boundaries mean, and how and when should you set them? Let's examine!

Emotional

Emotional boundaries are about respecting and protecting your feelings and personal energy. To set emotional boundaries, you must be aware of how full your emotional battery is. These boundaries may shift or change throughout the day, week, or month.

> **An emotional boundary might sound like this:**
>
> * I can't talk about this right now. I will let you know when I am ready.
>
> * I am having a difficult time. Do you think we can talk about it?
>
> * I feel hurt when you criticize me when I share my feelings and thoughts. I need you to respect my feelings.
>
> * Those words are hurtful, so I am stopping this conversation until we are calmer.

Time

Time boundaries protect your time! Your time is valuable and shouldn't be spent on things or people that drain your battery. Setting time boundaries allows you to focus on what's a priority and prevents you from overcommitting.

> **A time boundary might sound like this:**
>
> ★ I would love to go to the park with you, but I have to finish my science homework. Can we meet another day?
>
> ★ It would be fun to audition for the school play, but I am already signed up to help with the school newspaper and volunteer at the local library, so I can't do it this time.
>
> ★ I have to leave to babysit in half an hour and need time to get ready. Can I call you back tonight after eight?
>
> ★ I wish I could go to the party, but I have already committed to going to my friend's football game that night. Maybe next time!

Material

Material boundaries exist to protect your belongings or items you are utilizing. These boundaries also apply to money. It's ok not to share everything you have all the time. Material boundaries also establish the rules people must follow when borrowing something of yours.

> **A material boundary might sound like this:**
>
> * No, I'm sorry, but you can't have that chair. I'm waiting for a friend to join me in a few minutes.
>
> * Yes, you can borrow my blue dress, but please wash it before you return it to me.
>
> * I can't loan you my bike this weekend; I need it.
>
> * Yes, I'll give you $20, but please don't ask me for more and pay me back next week.

Intellectual

Intellectual boundaries are similar to emotional boundaries because they protect your thoughts, ideas, and beliefs. They require respect and a willingness to share and listen to others' ideas and beliefs. Intellectual boundaries may apply to politics, religion, current events, or artistic opinion.

An intellectual boundary might sound like this:

* I respect that you have a different opinion than mine, but I don't think this conversation was productive, so let's talk about something else.

* I understand you think differently than I do, but I ask that you respect me and refrain from using those kinds of words in front of me.

* I can see you don't like my idea for the group presentation, but you could have used kinder words.

Intimacy

Intimacy boundaries are those you establish with other people regarding your body. These boundaries determine who you will hug, shake hands with, or kiss. An intimacy boundary also concerns your personal space, such as standing a few feet from someone you don't know well or leaving space between you and the person in front of you in line at the store.

An intimacy boundary might sound like this:

* I feel uncomfortable with you standing this close to me. Could you please back up a few feet?

* I would prefer not to hug, please. How about a high five?

* I like you a lot but am not ready to kiss you yet.

* Take your hand off my back; it makes me uncomfortable.

Physical

Physical boundaries involve your physical energy levels and abilities. Like intimacy boundaries, they may also involve physical touches or sensations.

> **A physical boundary might sound like this:**
>
> * It is nice to meet you. I'm not a hug person, but I'll give you a fist bump. But I am not shaking hands right now because I don't want to get sick.
>
> * Your music is hurting my ears. Could you please lower the volume?
>
> * I would love to hang out, but I am really tired today. Maybe tomorrow.
>
> * I need to stop working on this and get something to eat.

Why You Shouldn't Feel Guilty for Saying No

We all want to please people and to make others happy; it is an inherent human trait that comes from wanting to feel a sense of belonging to a community. However, you should never feel guilty for putting yourself and your well-being first.

Boundaries are not selfish; they protect your mental and physical well-being. When you establish and enforce boundaries, you demonstrate self-respect, which means others will respect you, too!

It is also OK for your boundaries to shift and change in some cases, particularly emotional and physical because these boundaries are most likely to shift with your energy and emotional levels.

Boundaries promote mental well-being, physical health, self-esteem, and relationships with others. They also protect material belongings and time and prevent conflicts.[17]

Friendship Test

True friends will respect your boundaries, and you will respect theirs. If you have a friend who makes you feel uncomfortable or who lowers your self-esteem, put them to the friendship test by establishing a new boundary.

Keep in mind that a friend might be doing something that upsets you or drains you emotionally without their knowing it, especially if you've never said anything before or have no boundaries established.

So, set a boundary the next time they say or do something that causes you to feel upset, frustrated, or diminished. "Hey, I don't know if you realize it, but when you say that to me, it really hurts my feelings. I need you to stop saying that to me, please." Or, "This is the third time you've borrowed a book of mine and returned it with a stain. The next time you borrow a book, please be more careful, or I won't be able to loan books to you anymore."

If your friend is a real friend, they will respect your boundaries. They might not be a true friend if they become defensive, upset, or make excuses.

Define Your Boundaries

Think about some things in your day to day life or relationships making you uncomfortable or draining your energy. Write them down in column 1. Next to it, in column 2, add what new boundary you would like to set either with yourself or others.

Energy Drainers	Boundaries

REMEMBER! Boundaries aren't selfish; they are essential for strong relationships and physical and mental well-being. Boundaries protect your time, emotions, intimate and physical space and abilities, intellectual thoughts, and material belongings. People who care about you and respect you will also respect your boundaries.

DEALING WITH "MEAN GIRLS" AND PEER PRESSURE

> *"Calling somebody else fat won't make you any skinnier. Calling someone stupid doesn't make you any smarter."*
> ~ **Cady (Lindsay Lohan)**, Mean Girls

The opening quote of this chapter comes from the popular 2004 film *Mean Girls*, which starred Lindsay Lohan, Rachel McAdams, Amanda Seyfried, and Lacey Chabert.

The movie is a comedy but accurately depicts how mean girls can be to one another. Females are hard-wired to compete against one another. After all, our ancient ancestors had to compete to find a suitable mate.[18] Throughout history, women have competed with one another to find a suitable husband; to marry "well." It wasn't until after WWII and the feminist revolution of the 1970s and '80s that women began working outside the home and becoming self-sufficient. While you won't be marrying anytime soon, this is still a trait that can naturally occur as a teen.

Despite the headway women have made in the world, the hard wiring to compete hasn't changed. It is human nature to want to be the best and have the best. Unfortunately, that's not always the best way to live or interact with others.

Healthy competition is beneficial; it makes you work harder, learn new skills, and can create opportunities for self-improvement.

However, being mean and spiteful to hurt someone's feelings or in an attempt to make oneself feel better benefits no one.

So, what can you do if you have a "mean girl" in your life? How can you avoid interacting with them and maintain your self-esteem? It starts with being confident in yourself and what matters most to you.

> **DID YOU KNOW?** *Saturday Night Live* alum Tina Fey wrote *Mean Girls*. It was so popular that it has since been turned into a hit Broadway musical. The pop-rock musical premiered in Washington, DC, in 2017 and opened on Broadway in 2018. It started touring the US in 2003. The musical won an Outer Critics Circle Award for Outstanding Book of a Musical (the script).

Don't Let Them Bring You Down

A mean girl's goal is to make you feel bad about yourself; it sounds easier than it is, but don't let her. Mean girls are bullies. They may not throw punches or physically accost you, but spreading gossip, name-calling, and teasing are also forms of bullying. Whether it happens in person or online (cyberbullying), these actions can feel hurtful.

When confronted with a mean girl, the most powerful thing you can do is not to show her that her actions or words affect you. Even if inside you are boiling mad, feel like crying, or are embarrassed, if you give a bully little to no response, you've taken their power away, and eventually, they will stop and leave you alone.

If a bully can't make you feel bad, then there's no fun in it for them. Of course, mean and negative comments can hurt, but it is also essential to remind yourself that you are the only person who can decide how you feel. Only you can decide your value.

"No one can make you feel inferior without your consent."
~ Eleanor Roosevelt, First Lady of the United States (1933-1945)

However, it can be challenging to remind yourself of your incredible value and fantastic worth to others when a mean girl is in your ear. So, what can you do to maintain a positive mindset?

Tips to Maintain A Positive Mindset

Do something kind for someone else
Acts of kindness, such as complimenting someone or helping a person in need, will also make you feel better.

Smile and laugh
Research shows that smiling gives us more enjoyment than a piece of chocolate and automatically boosts our mood.

Journal
Journaling helps you organize your thoughts, express your feelings, and provides time to reflect. As you journal, write down a few things about yourself that you like and are grateful for.

Go for a walk
Physical exercise boosts our mood and energy. If walks aren't your thing, try yoga, stretching, strength training, or playing your favorite sport.

Listen to music
Music can improve your mood by lowering anxiety and symptoms of depression. Music also boosts your heart's health and reduces fatigue!

Talk to someone
Talking to a friend, trusted adult, or family member can help alleviate negative feelings, and they can remind you how awesome you are!

Some teasing and unpleasant remarks are an unfortunate part of adolescence, but bullying is different; bullying is a persistent, purposeful, harmful behavior.

Bullying is not something you should allow or tolerate. Tell a parent, teacher, or other trusted adult if you are being bullied. According to the Anti-Bullying Alliance, "Bullying is the repetitive, intentional hurting of one person or group by another person or group, where the relationship involves an imbalance of power. Bullying can be physical, verbal, or psychological."[19]

Your peers and friends are an important and valuable source of information and ideas and make up most of your social life. However, these influences aren't always positive, especially if you're being encouraged to act like a mean girl yourself or participate in activities you usually wouldn't. This type of influence is called peer pressure, and while challenging, there are ways you can resist and stay true to yourself!

Stay Strong: Resisting Peer Pressure

The urge to fit in and be approved by friends and peers is powerful during your teen years. Our friends often influence us to do and try new things. Sometimes, this is positive; your best friend convinces you to try out for the school play, and you get a great part, or your friend on the softball finally convinces you to watch one of her games, and you realize how much fun it is.

However, peer pressure isn't always positive. Negative peer pressure is people at a party trying to convince you to try a beer, a friend telling you to put the candy bar at 7-Eleven in your pocket and walk out, or the girl at your lunch table teasing the new girl and egging you to join in.

Ignoring or not giving in to peer pressure can be extremely difficult. It is common in human society to want to fit in, and often, the more people involved, the more potent the pressure feels. Sometimes, we get caught up in the action without even realizing it. Have you ever attended a high-energy concert or exciting sports event with everyone cheering and screaming? When a community of people comes together to participate in the same action, it's called collective effervescence.[20]

It's the exciting feeling you get on New Year's Eve when everyone starts counting down or at a 4th of July parade with patriotic music and everyone waving flags. The opposite side of collective effervescence is called mob mentality. Mob mentality is when an individual is influenced by a larger group of people.[21] Not all peer pressure is mob mentality, but all mob mentality is peer pressure.

You can face pressure from one individual or a group, but oftentimes, it is harder to say no to a group than an individual. So, what can you do when facing peer pressure and wanting to say no?

How to Say No: Directly and Indirectly

Sometimes, it will feel easy to say no. Let's say your friend wants you to go ziplining with them for their birthday but you are terrified of heights. You should have no problem saying, "No, that's not for me, but have fun! I'll meet you afterward." Other times, it's not so easy. Imagine your best friend wants to stay out late at a party and asks you to pretend she's at your house if her parents call. You know it's wrong and might get you in trouble, too. This situation might require a little more careful navigation.

Direct Ways to Say No

- Say "no thanks" or "not for me." If you feel confident, this is the easiest way!

- Back up a "no" with a positive statement. For example, "No, I'm not interested in that, but it seems like something you'll enjoy, so I hope you have fun!"

- Practice saying no to yourself in the mirror or for smaller boundaries. Once it becomes a habit to say no to things you don't like or don't want, saying it for the bigger things will be much easier.

- Plan responses in advance. If you know that a situation might occur, practice what you might say ahead of time. For example, if your friend has asked you three times to work with her on her science fair project and you haven't, it's likely not something that interests you. Practice what you'll say when she asks for the fourth time so you can confidently say no.

- Use the buddy system. There is power in numbers. Both collective effervescence and mob mentality tell us this, so have a friend with you when you need to say no to a situation.

Indirect Ways to Say No

- Avoid stressful situations in the first place. If you know mean girls will be at your friend's sleepover, don't go. If you know the boy who's been pressuring you to go out will be at the park that afternoon, head to the library instead.

- Volunteer a better idea. If you're being pressured into something negative, find a better solution. For example, if your sister is pressuring you to take $20 from your dad's wallet so you can go to Starbucks, you could say, "How about we volunteer to do the dishes for a week and ask Dad for the $20?"

- Write in a journal. Journals are a safe spot to store your thoughts and work out your feelings about a situation before making a decision.

- Speak to parents or other adults for support. If you're being pressured into a potentially dangerous or illegal situation, trust your parents or another trusted adult for help. They can offer guidance and probably solutions you didn't think of alone.

- Use humor to deflect pressure or attention. Humor is an excellent way to deflect uncomfortable situations; just make sure the humor isn't directed at anyone or harmful to anyone.

- Move away from the situation. Simply leave. You don't always have to respond verbally, so if something is happening that makes you uncomfortable, leave.

- Ask questions. If you're unsure if you want to participate in something, start asking questions. Why do they think this is a good idea? What do they hope to gain by doing this? Perhaps by asking questions, you'll also help the other person make a positive choice!

Create a Shield of Self-Worth and hang it in your bedroom to remind yourself how amazing you are. Saying no to peer pressure and being the target of mean girls might make you doubt your self-worth; your shield will be a positive reminder that you are in control of how you feel and act.

Shield of Self-Worth

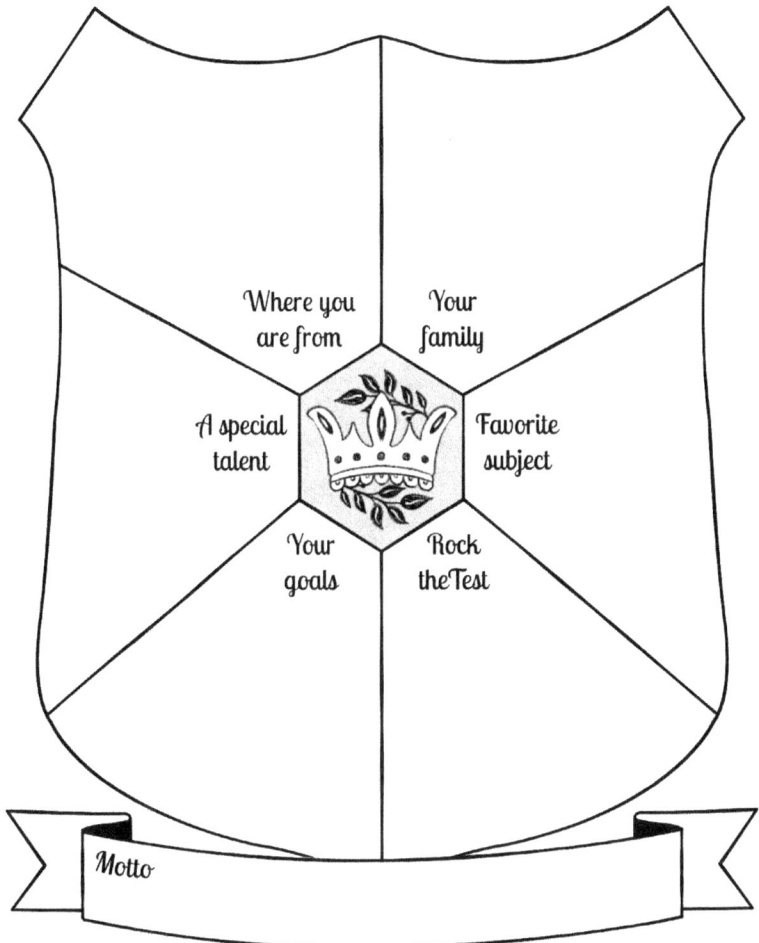

Motto
A short phrase that shows what you believe and stand for.

IDEAS
* Stay cool — no need to stress!
* Keep going — something awesome might just be ahead
* Progress not perfection.
* First things first, and one thing at a time.
* I give my best — that's what counts!
* You can always choose calm, even when it's hard.
* Real happiness starts with you, not stuff.

"Nobody has a better vision of who you are than yourself."
~ Sheryl Crow, Grammy Award-winning musical artist and songwriter

REMEMBER! Mean girls are mean because they don't value themselves and have low self-esteem. People who feel good about themselves don't feel the need or desire to put others down. If you're the target of a mean girl, as tricky as it may be, try to ignore her and focus on why you're incredible. If you're feeling pressure from mean girls to act a certain way so you fit in, but it goes against what you feel is right or true, it is OK to say no. You can say no directly or indirectly, whatever works best for you. Staying true to who you are is the ultimate goal.

HOW TO HANDLE CRITICISM AND REJECTION LIKE A BOSS

"I think the hardest part about being a teenager is dealing with other teenagers — the criticism and the ridicule, the gossip and rumors."
~ **Beverly Mitchell, actress**

Nobody enjoys being criticized — it never feels great to have your actions, efforts, or words picked apart. But both constructive and negative criticism are part of life.

As a tween or teen, dealing with criticism can feel especially tough because you're still figuring out who you are and what you're good at. But here's the important thing to remember: **criticism doesn't mean you're bad at something or a failure.**

There are different types of criticism, and the first step in handling it is learning to tell the difference between **helpful** and **hurtful** feedback.

If it's mean or negative with no purpose other than to make you feel bad — you can let it go. It's not worth your energy.

But if it's positive or constructive criticism, it's worth paying attention to. That kind of feedback can help you grow, improve, and become even more confident in what you do.

DID YOU KNOW?

One of the main reasons people criticize others is because they feel intimidated. They might be reacting to your skills, intelligence, success, or appearance. Criticism often comes from insecurity or an unmet need the person is experiencing. They may be trying to feel more important or covering up their own anger or hurt feelings by taking it out on someone else.

Occasionally, harsh criticism can come from someone with poor social skills or someone who genuinely means well and believes they're being helpful or knowledgeable about the situation.[22]

Try to take criticism with a grain of salt and reflect on whether what the person is saying has any value — or if it's simply negative and hurtful.

Types of Criticism

There are many types of criticism; some psychologists argue that there are upwards of eighteen to twenty or more different kinds of criticism! That's a lot of criticism. However, not all will apply to you as a teen, nor will you face all these different kinds in your life. Nonetheless, being familiar with different types of criticism that could come your way prepares you to deal with the associated feelings.

So, what are all these different types of criticism? Let's examine a few you might face as a teen.

Positive Types of Criticism

- **Constructive Criticism:** Constructive criticism is a valuable tool for affecting positive change in someone or something else. For example, your teacher might offer constructive criticism with suggestions on how you could improve your next essay.

- **Actionable Criticism:** Actionable criticism aims to solve a problem. It provides actionable steps. For example, if you need to improve a dance step, your teacher might give you exercises and pointers you can practice to improve.

- **Factual Criticism:** Factual criticism points out information that's incorrect or incomplete. For example, let's say a friend confidently tells the class that the Great Wall of China is the only man-made object you can see from space. While many people believe this, it's actually **not true** — astronauts have said the wall is very hard to see from space without special equipment. You could gently let your friend know that a lot of people think that too, but it's a common myth. That way, you're correcting the fact without making them feel bad.

- **Self-Criticism**: Self-criticism is healthy and positive if you reflect realistically. However, it is not uncommon to be overly critical of things you perceive as "flaws" or embarrassing mistakes. You might feel insecure and critical of yourself if you forgot your lines in the school play. Good self-criticism would look like acknowledging you didn't dedicate as much time to rehearsal as you should and reminding yourself to rehearse more next time. Negative self-criticism would look like calling yourself stupid and making the assumption you will never be cast in a role again. Self-criticism can be used as a tool for harm or self-improvement.

Negative Types of Criticism

- **Moral or Biased Criticism:** Moral criticism is based on a person's personal values, beliefs, or opinions. These are often influenced by things like religion, culture, or how someone was raised. For example, someone might have strong opinions about how others dress, what they eat, or the products they use.

A person who eats meat might be criticized by a vegetarian — or the other way around — because of their different beliefs.

- **Personal Criticism:** Personal criticism targets who you are, not what you've done. For example, someone might criticize you just for having red hair, or you might not be chosen for the lead role in a play because the director thinks you're too young. In situations like these, the criticism isn't about your actions or abilities — it's about something personal, which can feel especially hurtful.

- **Self-Criticism**: Self-criticism becomes harmful when you focus only on what you did "wrong" or how you "failed," without thinking about how to improve or learn from the situation. Sometimes, self-criticism isn't even necessary — especially if you didn't actually do anything wrong. You might just feel like you did because of something someone else said or did that made you doubt yourself.

When facing criticism, decide which category it falls into and whether it is positive and helpful or negative and can be discarded.

Types of Criticism

 **POSITIVE**

 **NEGATIVE**

- **Constructive Criticism:**
  Provides suggestions for improvement.

- **Actionable Criticism:**
  Offers specific steps to solve a problem.

- **Factual Criticism:**
  Gently informs and corrects misinformation.

- **Self-Criticism:**
  A tool for self improvement when done in a healthy way.

- **Moral Criticism:**
  Based on personal values and beliefs.

- **Personal Criticism:**
  Targets a person's characteristics or traits.

- **Self-Criticism:**
  Harmful when focused solely on perceived failures without considering improvement or learning.

Women Who Didn't Allow Rejection to Stop Them

Many successful women have faced failure, rejection, or harsh criticism — but they didn't let it stop them. Fashion designer Vera Wang and pop star Lady Gaga are just two examples of women who kept going, even when things didn't go their way.

Let's look at a few more stories of women who turned rejection into motivation and went on to achieve incredible success.

- **Jessica Alba** (Actress and Business Owner): Jessica Alba started as an actress in Hollywood but spent years being rejected by potential business partners before she launched her now best-selling brand, Honest Company. She said people only saw her as a pretty girl in a bathing suit, not someone with a brain and a vision.

- **Roxane Gay** (Bestselling Author): In an interview, Roxane Gay said, "Rejection is the most common thing a writer can experience." But despite numerous rejections, she kept trying and became a *New York Times* bestselling author with her collection of essays titled *Bad Feminist*.

- **Margaret Cho** (Comedian): Margaret has talked candidly about facing rejection time and again, but she said she doesn't let all the little rejections or failures faze her. She says she lives to enjoy each day and doesn't give up. If she's rejected, she looks at the situation and tries to approach it differently the next time.

- **Misty Copeland** (Dancer for the American Ballet Theater): In 2015, Misty Copeland became the first African-American to be promoted to principal dancer. But before that, she faced years of rejection. At various points in her career, she has been told she is too short, too curvy, her skin tone isn't the right color, and that she started dancing too late to succeed.

- **Sofia Coppola** (Film Director): Sofia Coppola is an award-winning filmmaker, but she has faced a lot of rejection in a field dominated by men. She's never been afraid to push the boundaries of filmmaking and has received harsh criticism of her work at times. Nonetheless, she has an Academy Award, Golden Globe, and Cannes Film Festival Award.

Your Three-Step Rejection Plan: Feel it, Learn from it, Move on Stronger

Rejection is going to happen. There is no way to avoid it in life unless you live in a bubble and never leave your home. Whether you are dealing with rejection from someone you asked on a date, rejection from your hoped-for college, rejection from the sports team or school play, or one of life's many other situations, we can't avoid rejection, but we can create a plan to better deal with it.

Use this Three-Step Rejection Plan the next time you face rejection so you can learn and move forward.

> *"Forget what hurt you, but never forget what it taught you."*
> ~ **Shannon L. Alder, writer and speaker**

- Feel It: Sit with your feelings. Give yourself time to feel and process whatever emotions come from the rejection: embarrassment, frustration, anger, sadness, envy, disappointment, fear, anxiousness, hopelessness, etc. There are negative emotions, but there are no bad emotions, meaning every emotion you feel is valid and OK.

- Learn From It: What opportunities are there to learn from the rejection?

  » Be honest with yourself — was there anything you could have done differently? If not, let that part go. Sometimes rejection is out of your control. Maybe the casting director wanted someone with brown hair, and you're blonde. Maybe the person you like is already dating someone else. Maybe there were 2,000 scholarship applicants and only five spots.

  » But if there *is* something you could change, ask yourself: What is it — and is the change realistic? Maybe you were cut from the basketball team because you made fewer free throws than the other players. That's something you can work on with practice. Maybe the school newspaper rejected your article because the topic didn't fit. You could ask the editor what topics they're looking for and try again.

  » Whether or not there's something to change, take a moment to reflect:
    ▫ What did you learn about yourself?
    ▫ Did you discover that you can manage your nerves with enough preparation?

- Did you realize you're more resilient than you thought?
- Did you learn that rejection doesn't mean you have less value, talent, or potential?

• Move on Stronger: You've felt your feelings, you've reflected on what you can learn — and now it's time to move on. But not just move on...**move on stronger**. Dwelling on what happened won't change it. Instead, acknowledge how you feel, take what you've learned,  and let that growth shape you. Every time you grow from an experience — even a tough one — you become stronger, wiser, and more confident in who you are.

REMEMBER! Criticism and rejection do not equal failure. Rejection means this wasn't the right time or place for you and your unique talents. So keep going and keep trying. As the saying goes, when one door closes, another door opens. When rejection and criticism happen, feel your way through it, learn from it, and grow stronger so that you're better prepared the next time you're faced with a similar situation. And remember, there are some things outside your control; learn to let go of those things and focus on what's next.

PART 3:

TAKE ACTION AND BE BRAVE (EMPOWERMENT IN ACTION)

10

HOW TO GO AFTER WHAT YOU WANT (EVEN WHEN IT'S SCARY!)

"How we handle our fears will determine where we go with the rest of our lives. To experience adventure or to be limited by the fear of it."
~ *Judy Blume, author*

Fears come in all shapes and sizes. Some are huge and can stop you in your tracks — like spotting a giant spider in the bathroom and refusing to go in there for a week. Others are small, like wondering if your teacher will approve your essay topic because you're really excited to write about it.

The level of fear we feel doesn't always match how risky something actually is. For example, fear of spiders is one of the most common fears in the world — even though in most places, the spiders we come across aren't venomous or harmful at all.

On the flip side, most of us don't think twice about getting in a car, even though driving is way more dangerous than flying. Statistically, you have a 1 in 654 chance of dying in a car crash as a passenger — but only a 1 in 9,821 chance of dying in a commercial plane crash. That's a pretty big difference!

So does knowing that flying is safer make people less afraid of it? Maybe.

Sometimes, learning more about what you're afraid of can help reduce the fear. But even with all the facts in the world, fear of failure, rejection, embarrassment, or getting hurt can still hold you back from going after what you want.

If you're someone who often shies away from things because of fear — whatever that fear may be — this chapter is for you.

Your new mantra? **"Fear means go!"**

> **DID YOU KNOW?**
>
> Pop star, actress, and mental health advocate **Selena Gomez** has openly talked about her struggles with **anxiety, panic attacks, and depression**. At one point, her anxiety became so overwhelming that she had to cancel part of her tour and take time off to focus on her mental health.
>
> Selena didn't try to hide what she was going through. Instead, she worked with professionals, surrounded herself with support, and spoke out to help others feel less alone. One of her most powerful messages?
>
> "If you are broken, you do not have to stay broken."
>
> Selena used therapy, creativity, and self-care to get back to doing what she loves most — performing, creating music, and using her platform to support others.

Fear Means Go!

Luckily, most of us won't face the kind of public pressure or emotional weight Selena has — but fear can still hold us back in powerful ways.

Whether it's stage fright, fear of failure, or the worry that you're not "good enough," those thoughts can stop you from trying — and from growing.

If you constantly tell yourself, *No, I can't,* you'll never discover just how strong and capable you really are.

Fear is a natural, evolutionary response designed to keep our ancestors safe. It helped protect early humans from poisonous plants, dangerous animals, risky situations, and even rival tribes that might try to take their resources.

The problem? While human life has changed a *lot* in the last five thousand years since written language began, our brains still have some very **primitive parts**. Those old parts of the brain still react to fear in the same way — whether it's a tiger in the bushes or… auditioning for a solo or applying to your dream school.

Some fear is actually helpful. It can **keep us safe**, **make us think carefully**, and **stop us from making rash decisions**. But too much fear can hold us back from doing things we *can* do—and even *want* to do.

So from now on, when you feel afraid of something that really matters to you, remind yourself: ☞ **Fear means go.**

But how do you "go" when you're scared? Here are some tips!

Tips to Overcome Minor (Or Even Medium) Fears

★ Educate yourself.
The more you know about a person, situation, experience, process, place, event, etc., the less fear you'll have. Are you afraid of applying to your dream college because you think you won't get in? Learn everything you can about the admissions process. Talk to people at the school, people who've applied, read the website cover to cover, etc.

★ Find your inner confidence.
This book discusses confidence extensively because confidence is central to being the best version of yourself and attaining your goals. Remind yourself why you can do this, and remember that a failure or "no" this time doesn't mean the answer will always be no.

★ Meditation and breathing exercises.
Engaging in mindfulness can ease anxiety and help you face your fears. There are many free meditation apps, like Calm, or videos online on YouTube. For example, one popular video is "10 Minute Meditation to Release Stress & Anxiety" by the YouTuber Lavendaire. Regular meditation practice can significantly reduce stress and anxiety, leading to a less fearful you more of the time!

★ Practice and exposure.
Whatever you're afraid of doing, practice it as much as possible—whether it's sports, music, writing, making online content, or petting a dog! The more exposure and experience you have with something, the less frightening it becomes.

★ Visualize your end goal.
What is it that overcoming your current fear will help you accomplish? Is it so you can win the state spelling bee or make the varsity soccer team? Think about why facing the fear is crucial and how not facing it likely results in you not achieving your goal.

What's the Worst That Could Happen?

The worst thing that can happen in any situation is that you never even try — and miss out on reaching your goals. But when we say "the worst," that's not usually where our brains go.

Instead, we imagine things like embarrassment, rejection, shame, sadness, or envy. Sometimes so many of these negative feelings overlap that we get stuck in a kind of thought paralysis — we overthink so much that we freeze and don't act at all.

Broadway and film star Idina Menzel has shared a story about her final audition for the role of Elphaba in the original Broadway cast of *Wicked*. At the time, her career had stalled after *RENT*, despite earning a Tony nomination, and she was hoping *Wicked* would be her big break.

But during her audition, right at the climactic final note of *Defying Gravity*, her voice cracked. She felt scared and angry — but she didn't stop. Instead, she cursed under her breath, took a deep breath, and sang the note again — this time, perfectly.

Later, the director told her that moment was one of the reasons she got the part. She didn't crumble — she pushed through, and that courage stood out. Since then, her career has taken off, and she even voiced one of Disney's most iconic characters, singing "Let It Go" in *Frozen*.

That audition fail — her voice cracking — was probably one of the worst things she could've imagined happening...and it did happen. But she kept going anyway.

So, what's the worst that could happen to you? You strike out every time at bat? You ask someone if you can join their group and get rejected or laughed at? You trip during your dance audition? Your dream college says no?

Now try this: **Take that fear and exaggerate it to the extreme.**

Not only do you strike out — you also spill something down your pants that looks *very* unfortunate. Then you trip over your bat, twist your ankle, and your coach yells at you while everyone's laughing. Sounds ridiculous, right?

Sounds dramatic, right? That's the point.

This technique is actually based on a real mental health strategy called cognitive defusion, used in a type of therapy called ACT (Acceptance and Commitment Therapy). When you take your scary thoughts and exaggerate them, your brain starts to realize they're not as serious or realistic as they felt at first. Studies have shown this technique helps reduce anxiety and makes those thoughts feel less powerful.[23]

So next time you're afraid of "the worst that could happen," try this trick. You might find that even if something goes wrong, it's not nearly as bad as your brain made it seem. And the best part? You still tried — and that's a win all on its own.

> **REMEMBER!**
>
> Reward rarely comes without risk. Taking risks doesn't always mean danger. In fact, the kind of risks we're talking about — like trying something new, speaking up, or putting yourself out there — are usually only risky in the sense that you might fail or feel embarrassed.
>
> And while failure and embarrassment aren't exactly fun, they shouldn't stop you from going after the things you want.
>
> If you want to build your courage, start with micro-bravery. That means doing small, regular acts of bravery — things that stretch you just a little bit outside your comfort zone. Over time, these small steps help reduce your fear and make trying new things feel way less scary.

What other acts of micro-bravery can you think of to try?

Weekly Courage Challenge

Commit yourself to a weekly courage challenge for the next several weeks. Choose one item from the list below or write your own. The goal is to put your courage to the test with these micro-bravery acts and overcome fears through exposure and practice!

- Say hello to someone you admire but have never talked to before.

- Attend a meeting for a school club or organization that interests you.

- Write an email to an author or artist that inspires you. Send it anonymously if you prefer.

- Speak up in a class you are typically quiet during.

- Watch a movie or read a book you have never seen before.

- Try a new hobby.

- Stand up for someone or something you think is being treated unfairly.

- Apologize for something you did wrong or a mistake you made.

- Ask an adult to help you face a personal fear: fear of dogs, snakes, public speaking, heights, etc.

- Try something new: visit a new (but safe) part of your city or town with your parents, leave your phone at home while you take a walk, eat a new cuisine you have never tried before, or try a new outfit combination.

- Say yes to a social situation that makes you a little nervous, such as a big party, trivia night, or singing karaoke.

11

FACING FEARS AND PUSHING PAST SELF-DOUBT

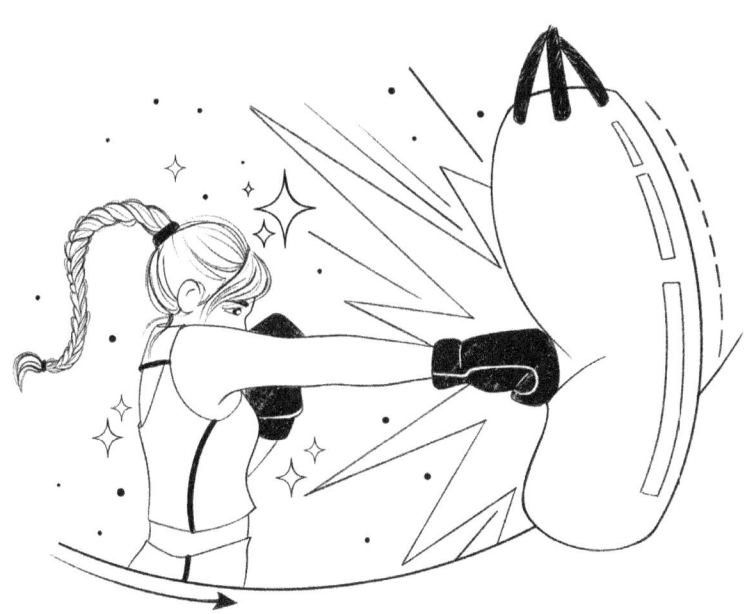

"Doubt kills more dreams than failure ever will."
~ Suzy Kassem, artist

The quote above is simple — but so true. You may have also heard the phrase, "You miss 100 percent of the shots you don't take," often linked to hockey star Wayne Gretzky. Whether or not he was the first to say it, the message is clear: **if you don't try, you can't succeed**.

That brings us back to Suzy Kassem's quote at the top. If you let doubt take over, you might not even try — and that means you'll never know what you could've achieved.

Want to learn to ice skate? You have to step onto the ice. Dream of going to university or college? You have to send in the application.

In Chapter 10, you learned how to take action even when you're scared. But sometimes, it's not just fear that gets in the way — it's doubt. And when doubt takes over your thoughts, it can be really hard to push past it.

Self-doubt often comes from past experiences or things other people have said to you. It grows when confidence is low — and it can be strong enough to freeze you in place, making you too scared to try.

But here's the good news: you can overcome self-doubt. It might take time, but it is absolutely possible.

> **DID YOU KNOW?**
>
> *Harry Potter* star Emma Watson (Hermione) has struggled with self-confidence and doubt since she first starred in the hit movie series. She has opened up about how she thought she wasn't pretty and felt uncomfortable having her picture taken. She strongly disliked seeing herself on magazine covers and billboards and has had to work through her feelings to build her confidence.

Self-Doubt: Where Does It Come From, and How Do We Get Rid of It?

A fear of spiders or snakes differs from a fear stemming from doubt. Our fear of physical things or experiences — like bugs, flying, or the ocean — may or may not come from life experiences, but more often, these fears stem from an irrational place and a lack of knowledge.

Self-doubt, on the other hand, often develops as we mature. So where does self-doubt come from — and how can we get rid of it, or at least make it smaller?

The Origins of Self-Doubt

Self-doubt results from a combination of places or experiences. Depending on the situation, it could result from one or several factors.

1. **Your Childhood:** How your parents, guardians, or other important adults spoke to and interacted with you as a young child could have influenced your level of confidence and self-doubt. Likewise, if you were a child who was allowed to take small risks, such as climbing on the monkey bars, walking home from school alone when old enough, or playing sports, you will also have lower levels of self-doubt.

2. **Past Experiences and Mistakes**: Past experiences — like times when you've failed, felt embarrassed, or made mistakes — can definitely impact your level of self-doubt. Trying something new (or trying again after a failure) can feel scary, especially if things didn't go well before. But while it can be challenging, it's not impossible to overcome that fear and build confidence again.

3. **Comparing Yourself to Others**: Comparing yourself to what you know or think you know about others can cause doubt and fear, especially in areas of competition like sports, drama, music, and academics.

4. **Fear of Success:** Fear of failure is a common reason for self-doubt, but so is fear of success! The fear is that if you succeed,

you won't be able to handle the challenge or responsibility that comes with it.

5. **Fear of the New or Unknown**: The less you know about something, the more scary it can feel. You might dream of traveling to Italy on a school trip this summer but also be terrified you won't be able to communicate with people, worry about getting lost, or be homesick.

Getting Rid of Fear Caused by Self-Doubt

Once you understand what's contributing to your self-doubt, you can start working through it — and begin facing new and exciting challenges with more confidence!

1. **Ask for Help:** It might seem simple, but many people avoid asking for help because they're afraid of looking "dumb" or unskilled. The truth is, asking for help is one of the best ways to learn and grow. If you need help — ask! That's how new skills are built.

2. **Ground Yourself:** Find something that calms your mind and helps you feel centered. Breathing exercises, meditation, listening to music, reading, journaling, being outside, or going for a walk are all great ways to ground yourself and feel more in control.

3. **Make a Pros and Cons List:** Whether you're afraid of failure, success, or something in between, writing out the pros and cons of each outcome can help. Seeing both the positives and negatives gives you a clearer, more balanced view of what might happen — and how you'd handle it.

4. **Stop Comparing Yourself to Others**: Comparing yourself to others can sometimes inspire you — but when it starts to make you feel "less than," it's time to stop. You're not going to look like Gigi Hadid if you want to be a model — but that's a good thing! You have your own unique look and personality to bring to the table. If you dream of being a CEO, it's fine to admire someone like Lauren Hobart (CEO of Dick's Sporting Goods), but remember — your path will be different from hers. And that's what makes it yours.

5. **Be Realistic about Where You Are in Your Journey:** Very few people wake up one day and instantly become a famous actor, a business success, or a sports star. Success takes time — and usually a few failures along the way. Be honest about where you are right now, what skills you still need to work on, who you can turn to for help, and what steps you need to take next. Whether your dream is big or small, every step counts.

Instant Bravery: Just Add Visualization

Bravery is often misdefined as not being afraid. But bravery doesn't mean you aren't scared; it means facing your fears and trying anyway. If you're in a situation where you need some instant bravery, whether to calm audition nerves or to take a big test, try out this instant bravery trick!

Neuro-associations are the associations our brains make with places, smells, tastes, sounds, etc. For example, the smell of a favorite dish might instantly remind you of your grandmother's kitchen, or the warmth of the sun on a spring day might take you back to playing outside with your friends.

These thoughts bring about emotions, which are pleasant ones in these scenarios. The same thought process can be applied to visualizing yourself as brave.

1. Think of something powerful, brave, and strong. It might be the ocean, a mountain, a superhero, or a big dog.

2. Next, think of other positive and powerful words you associate with this image. For our example, we'll use the ocean: massive, powerful, strong, beautiful, majestic, mighty, fearsome.

3. Now, create a short sentence describing your bravery as the ocean. For example, "Let's make waves!" or "I am mighty and powerful."

4. Visualize yourself as the ocean as you say these words. Stand taller, broaden your shoulders, and take a deep breath like the rolling waves.

While you can certainly use the ocean example here, this exercise will have more power if you choose imagery that is especially powerful and meaningful to you.

Pushing Fear Aside: Real Stories of Girls Who Overcame Self-Doubt

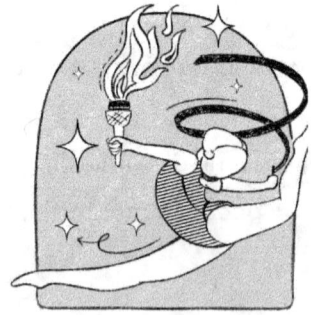

- **Simone Biles**–Olympic gold medalist Simone Biles has faced self-doubt over her body image due to criticism about her body shape and build. She's faced performance anxiety and other issues in the gymnastic world. Despite these issues and self-doubt, she's become one of the world's most famous and successful gymnasts.

- **Malala Yousafzai**—When Malala was fifteen, she was shot on a bus in Pakistan for attending school. She was already defying local authorities by attending school as a female. At seventeen, she became the youngest Nobel Peace Prize winner.

- **Bethany Hamilton**: Bethany is a surfer who, at the age of thirteen, was attacked by a fourteen-foot shark and lost her arm. Hamilton didn't let the accident stop her; once she recovered, she started surfing again and is also a public speaker.

> **REMEMBER!** Doubt and fear can come from your past, comparisons, and even the fear of success! Figuring out where your fear and self-doubt are coming from is the first step to overcoming them. Your self-doubt is linked to your confidence level. Asking for help, learning new skills, and not comparing yourself to others are three actions you can take to erase self-doubt.

TURNING SETBACKS INTO COMEBACKS

> *"Rock bottom became the solid foundation on which I rebuilt my life."*
> ~ **J.K. Rowling, author**

You should be so proud of yourself. Look — you're almost at the end of the book, and that deserves a big pat on the back!

You've learned so much already. Chapters 10 and 11 explored how to face your fears and overcome self-doubt so you can go after your goals and try new things.

But what happens when you do try and fail? What if you're struggling to bounce back? How do you become — and stay — resilient?

Like many personal growth skills, bouncing back from a setback takes mental strength, practice, and time.

Failure can make you feel discouraged. And it's not always about how *big* the failure is — it's more about how important the situation was to you. How you respond, and how you feel about it, shapes your resilience. And those feelings? They can change from day to day, or even hour to hour.

Getting knocked down during a soccer game might be a quick recovery — you can jump back up and keep running. But something like getting rejected from your dream school, losing a big competition, or failing an important test might take more time and a calmer mental space to process.

Still, every setback is a chance to grow. Bouncing back from failure is what turns setbacks into comebacks. Use these moments to learn, rise, and come back stronger than ever.

> **DID YOU KNOW?** At the age of twenty-two, US Marine Ramona Pierson was hit by a car while out for a run. She suffered one hundred and four broken bones and brain trauma and was in a coma for eighteen months. When she finally woke up, she discovered she was blind. Ramona didn't let this stop her from living life to her fullest ability. She regained some sight and began rock climbing and skiing, eventually qualifying for the US Paralympic and Olympic teams for cycling. Ramona went back to school, earned her PhD in Neuroscience, went back to work for the military, and started an educational startup. Now, that's a comeback!

Tips to Bounce Back

Like most emotional situations, learning to bounce back is often a matter of mind over matter. It means finding positive ways to reframe situations, turning failures into learning opportunities, and not judging yourself too harshly along the way.

The best way to practice bouncing back is to trust in yourself, listen, and seek support from those you trust most.

1. **Practice self-forgiveness:** No matter the setback, practice forgiving yourself. Allow yourself time with your feelings; negative feelings are natural during a setback, but don't wallow in them. Feelings will come and go as you heal, but do your best to forgive yourself so you can heal and move forward; trust yourself.

2. **Admit embarrassment or shame**: It is perfectly valid to feel embarrassment and shame after a setback, especially one that is public or well-known. Own those feelings as part of forgiving yourself. Most of the time, we dwell on situations that affect us directly for much longer than those that we merely witnessed or heard about. This means other people probably aren't dwelling on us. Get out of your head, stop worrying about what other

people think, and remind yourself it's okay to feel embarrassed, but it's time to move forward!

3. **Find perspective**: Take a step back and look at the bigger picture. Ask yourself:

   » Did what happened cause serious harm to anyone — physically or emotionally?

   » Did it damage anything important, like your home or personal belongings?

   » Will you lose your home, friends, or access to places you love because of it?

   If the answer to these questions is no, then — even if it's disappointing — what happened probably won't have any lasting impact on your life. Try asking yourself: *Will this matter in a week? A month? Five years?* In most cases, setbacks affect us for a short while — days, weeks, or maybe months — but they rarely cause chaos that lasts a lifetime. Talking it through with someone you trust can also help. Sometimes, hearing another person's perspective is all it takes to see the situation more clearly and feel more grounded.

4. **Reflect, learn, reset, and recalibrate**: Start by reflecting on what happened. Why do you think it happened? Could anything

have been done differently? Be honest with yourself — but not harsh. Next, figure out what you've learned (or still need to learn) in order to move forward or try again. Maybe you need more practice to sharpen a skill. Maybe you need to put your phone away while driving to stay focused. Or maybe you just need to spend more time proofreading your essays before turning them in. Then, reset your mindset so you can move on. This is where self-forgiveness and processing your emotions come in. You made a mistake — but now you're ready to grow from it. Finally, reset and plan your path forward. What now? What are the next steps you can take to try again, move forward, or even change directions entirely? Taking action — big or small — is what helps you turn a setback into progress.

Comeback Plan

Use the tips mentioned above to formulate a comeback plan. Sports teams, cities, companies, etc., create comeback plans when scores, quality of life, or sales begin to slump. You can use a similar technique to get things back on track after a personal setback.

There are several ways to create a setback plan; we'll outline some steps below to discover what works best for you.

1. **Accept the setback**: Step one is non-negotiable. You must accept what went wrong in order to move forward. Engage

in self-forgiveness, sit with the uncomfortable feelings, and admit it wasn't the outcome you hoped for; now, you're ready to move forward.

2. **Reanalyze and reset your goals**: Only you can decide what's next. Do you attempt the thing that caused the setback again? Do you move in another direction? Do you need to set smaller, more attainable goals before trying again? You might find advice by speaking to others who've faced similar situations or a trusted adult or friend. However, ultimately, only you can decide what's next and what your first step is to come back.

3. **Prioritize actions and goals:** Create an action plan by listing actionable steps and goals and then prioritize them. Perhaps step one is to spend thirty more minutes a day swimming laps, and the goal is that within a month, you speed up your qualifying time by two seconds. A secondary goal might be working with your coach on your arm movements to reduce friction. Whatever the case, figure out what's most important to you or what must happen before achieving the big goal.

4. **Find your support system**: Not everyone has a natural support system. Maybe your parents don't believe in your goal to become a musician, or you've recently moved to a new school and haven't made any friends yet. Achieving goals and bouncing back without a support system is challenging but not

impossible. Even if you can only find one or two people to turn to when things get tough, to bounce ideas off of, or to hang out with when you need a mental break, it will help you bounce back quicker.

5. **Stay positive:** Staying positive after a significant setback is difficult. However, maintaining a positive outlook will help you move forward and regroup. Try reframing negative thoughts. Reframing doesn't mean you make every situation 100 percent positive; it means you find something positive in every situation. You placed last in the race. Now you know what skills you need to improve for the next time. If you give up a sport that isn't making you happy anymore, you can focus on yourself and hang out with your other friends more. There's almost always a positive side to every situation.

6. **Celebrate**: Whatever small steps or achievements you've made or reached, celebrate! You've earned it. Celebrating even small goals helps you stay focused and motivated.

Failure, Not Defeat

Failure doesn't mean the end of the road. Many people experience major setbacks and still find a way to not only recover — but to move forward even further than before.

In Chapter 5, we mentioned fashion designer Vera Wang. She didn't make the US Olympic figure skating team, and that could have been the end of her dream. But instead of letting that define her, she took a different path and became one of the most successful women in the fashion industry. Does she still have regrets about not skating? Possibly. But she didn't let that one setback stop her from achieving success in another area of her life.

And she's not the only one! Many women and girls have faced huge obstacles, and gone on to do incredible things. Check out these inspiring stories:

Katy Perry: The thirteen-time Grammy-nominated pop star faced major setbacks early in her music career. At age twenty, she released a Christian music album under her real name, *Katy Hudson*. It only sold two hundred copies, and her record label went bankrupt. Over the next five years, she sold clothes and signed with two more  record companies — both deals fell through. But in 2006, she signed with Capitol Music Group and released her breakout hit "I Kissed a Girl," earning her first Grammy nomination.

Shannon Miller: Before she became one of the most decorated Olympic gymnasts in US history, Shannon Miller faced a serious setback. In 1992, she fell during training, dislocating her shoulder and breaking her elbow. After surgery and months of recovery, she refused to give up. She made the 1992 Olympic team and went on to win 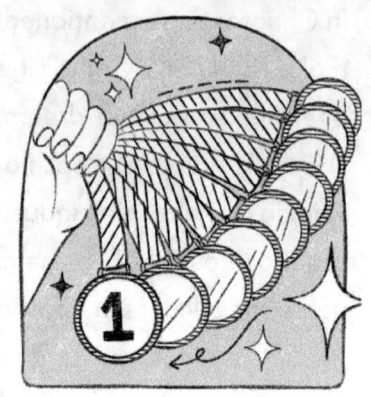 nine Olympic medals over her career. Today, she's a lawyer and advocate for women's health and sports.

Emily Blunt: British actress Emily Blunt grew up with a severe stutter that made it hard for her to speak. Speech therapy didn't seem to help — until one coach suggested she try acting. Surprisingly, when she performed using different voices or pretended to be someone else, her stutter disappeared. Acting gave her the confidence and voice she needed.
Today, she's one of the most successful actresses in Hollywood.

Martine Wright: Martine Wright lost both of her legs in the 2005 London bombings. The day before the attack, she had found out she was being considered for Great Britain's Olympic volleyball team. But she didn't let the tragedy stop her. She began training as a Paralympic athlete, and in 2012, she made the Paralympic Games squad. Today, she is a powerful voice for disabled athletes and a symbol of resilience.

REMEMBER! Failure is not the same as defeat. Defeat only happens when you give up; failure gives you the opportunity to try again or try something different. Bouncing back after failing is tough at times; the bigger the failure, the harder it can be, but those who fail and push their way forward again come back even brighter and stronger than before. When you face failure, develop a comeback plan so you are ready for next time. You might take two, six, or even twenty times to achieve your goal. But if you take each setback as a chance to learn, grow, and adjust, you'll continue to make progress!

HOW TO BE A LEADER IN YOUR OWN LIFE

"If I didn't fill my schedule with things I felt were important, other people would fill my schedule with things they felt were important."
~ **Melinda Gates, philanthropist and multimedia product designer**

You are the most powerful person in your life. Do you realize that now?

Aside from maybe your parents or best friend, there's probably no one who can stand up for you, empower you, and celebrate you as much as **you** can.

A central theme of this book has been about taking control of your life — through self-confidence, emotional growth, and problem-solving. Now, it's time to show others how it's done. Being a leader in your own life is one more powerful way to shape the direction your life takes.

A good leader does many things: A leader guides others in a positive, productive direction. A confident leader offers support and helpful feedback. And most importantly, a leader inspires others — to be better, do better, and treat others better.

But guess what? You don't need a title or an official role to be a leader.

You can lead just by being a positive role model among your friends and peers. If you want to lead your sports team, show up to practice on time, play with good sportsmanship, and work hard — without complaining.

If you want to lead in social situations, refuse to take part in bullying or gossip, show kindness and respect to others, and stay true to your values — even when it's not popular.

Being a leader isn't about bossing people around — it's about inspiring them. So, how do you become an inspiration to others, and what does it take to be a leader?

> **DID YOU KNOW?**
>
> History often overlooks powerful, female leaders. For example, have you ever heard of Zheng Yi Sao? She was the most successful pirate in history, with over seventy thousand pirates following her command. Another example is Mildred Harnack, who helped form and lead the largest underground resistance group against the Nazis in Berlin during World War II. And then there's Madame Nhu, the First Lady of South Vietnam from 1955 to 1963, who became a bold and influential political figure — fighting for women's legal rights in a time and place where that was incredibly rare.

How Being a Leader Could Look for You

Leaders inspire through positive actions and by being role models others want to follow.

Leading doesn't only happen when someone tells you you're in charge or assigns you as the captain of your sports team. It's not simply about giving orders or telling people what to do.

Of course, being a leader doesn't always mean making history like the women mentioned earlier. But a good leader can still have a powerful impact on someone's life — often without even realizing it. So even if you're not a pirate, a resistance organizer, or a powerful politician, you can still be a strong and influential leader.

Many great leaders — whether they're on big stages or in everyday life — share similar qualities and traits.

Traits of a Good Leader

- **Creativity**: Good leaders think outside the box. They can look at situations from multiple angles, problem-solve, and be willing to try new things and ideas.

- **Empathy:** Empathy is the ability to understand someone else's feelings. It differs from sympathy, which is feeling sorry or pity for someone else. People who can feel empathy try to view difficult situations through the eyes of the other person to gain an understanding of what they are feeling or going through.

- **Humility:** Humility is essential for leaders because a leader will not always be correct or have the best ideas. A good leader can admit when someone else has an idea that might work better than theirs. Good leaders share the trait for success with others.

- **Confidence:** Leaders display confidence in themselves and others. They have the confidence needed to make crucial decisions and show confidence in others by providing opportunities for them to shine.

- **Transparency:** Leaders don't hide their motives, desires, or strategies. They are open and honest about decisions and why they are made.

- **Delegation:** A successful leader knows when, how, and to whom to assign crucial roles and tasks. Good leaders know they cannot tackle every problem or situation themselves.

- **Compassion:** Compassion is an awareness and sympathy for others' struggles. Possessing compassion means a leader recognizes when someone may need a break, a change, or a listening ear.

- **Flexibility:** Strong leaders know that things don't always go as planned. They can think on their toes, make changes, and problem-solve when the unexpected happens.

- **Accountability:** Leaders need accountability to admit mistakes. Whether the mistake was directly theirs or the result of an action poorly delegated, a good leader can admit when some or all of the fault lies with them.

- **Respect:** Respect is critical in all our relationships because it opens the doors to successful communication. Showing respect to those you disagree with or dislike is a powerful tool for a leader.

How Can You Use These Traits Daily?

- **Creativity:** You're working on a group history project, and your group is stuck on how to present the material. You suggest using a PowerPoint with animated images and graphics, since you're good at design and think it will help keep your classmates engaged.

- **Empathy:** Your friend was just dumped by her boyfriend and says she wants to text his new girlfriend. You listen to your friend and empathize with her hurt and loneliness. You gently suggest that she process her thoughts and feelings before making any decisions she might regret later.

- **Humility:** You're the editor of your school's online newsletter and notice fewer people are reading and commenting on the articles. You call a team meeting, admit you're not sure what's going wrong, and ask the group to work together to come up with solutions.

- **Confidence:** You're directing the school drama club play, and someone disagrees with one of your casting choices. You calmly and clearly explain why you believe the person you chose is the best fit for the role, and express confidence in your decision.

- **Transparency:** As the netball team captain, you schedule two extra practice sessions a week before school each morning. You explain to your teammates specific skills the team needs to work on and why these skills are essential to the team's success.

- **Delegation:** You're volunteering at an animal shelter, and your usual dog-walking partner doesn't show up. There are too many dogs for you to safely walk alone. Instead of trying to do it all yourself, you ask another volunteer who isn't busy if they can help — delegating instead of overloading yourself and risking an accident.

- **Compassion:** You lent your friend your favorite sweatshirt, and her little brother spilled hot chocolate on it. She tried to get the stain out but couldn't. She returns it to you visibly upset. You can see she tried her best, and instead of getting mad, you let her know it's okay — accidents happen.

- **Flexibility:** You're hanging out with friends, and they all decide to take flirty photos to post on social media. You don't feel comfortable joining in, so you let them know you'd rather not take pictures — but you still offer to help them choose the best ones.

- **Accountability:** You borrow your friend's bike for the weekend to attend a concert in the park. On the way home, you hit a curb and bend the front wheel. You take responsibility, apologize, and offer to pay for the repair.

- **Respect:** You tried out for the school tennis team and found out this morning that you made it. A girl in your physics class also tried out but didn't make the cut. When she congratulates you, you thank her and take the opportunity to compliment her great backswing.

These are just a few ways you can show leadership in your daily life!

You can be a leader at home by taking on chores or responsibilities without being asked. You can set a positive example for your siblings by showing kindness, pitching in, and showing respect to your parents.

You can be a leader in your community by volunteering, getting a part-time job, babysitting, or offering to help elderly neighbors with yard work.

Not every leadership situation will require every quality. So when the opportunity to lead comes up, think about which traits will help the most — and use them to make a positive difference.

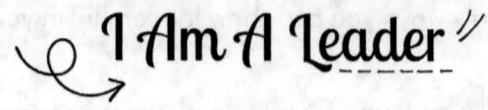

I Am A Leader

Being a leader is more natural for some people than others, but all effective leaders reflect and think about their actions and choices. Use the activity below to reflect on a recent or upcoming leadership opportunity.

What is/was the leadership opportunity?

Which leadership traits apply here?

Why?

Which traits I find challenging?	Why?

Which traits I find easiest to apply?	Why?

How did this leadership opportunity make me feel?

REMEMBER! Leaders have many different qualities that make them effective — but you don't need to use all of them at once or all the time.

Being a leader in your own life means setting a positive example when it matters, whether or not you're in an official leadership role. Sometimes, simply doing the right thing or helping others is leadership in action.

THE POWER OF LIFTING UP OTHER GIRLS, NOT COMPETING WITH THEM

"There is no limit to what we, as women, can accomplish."
~ Michelle Obama, First Lady of the United States, 2009–2017

Now that you're a total girlboss when it comes to handling mean girls and peer pressure, let's talk about what it really means to be a girl's girl.

We know that girls and women have a long history of competing against one another. But we also know it doesn't have to be that way; girls can be an incredible support system for each other, especially when they band together!

To stop competing *against* other girls and start cheering them on, the first step is to stop seeing them as your competition. Yes — healthy competition is great. It pushes you to grow and do your best. But the trick is to see the *goal* or *achievement* as what you're competing with — not the other people aiming for it.

If you give it your all — work hard, stay focused, and do your best — then the outcome is out of your hands. And if you start viewing other girls as sources of inspiration (not rivals), you'll experience more confidence, clearer thinking, and way less stress!

DID YOU KNOW?

Scientific research shows that women who have strong, supportive, and healthy relationships with other females tend to live longer. When women or teen girls spend time with their female friends, their brains release the "feel-good" hormone oxytocin.[24] That's a powerful reason to seek out female friendships that build you up!

The Benefits of Female Friendships

Friends of all kinds are beneficial, assuming the friendships are healthy and supportive, because true friendships are based on respect, kindness, and compatibility. However, science and psychology have shown that women reap specific benefits from healthy female friendships.

Be a True Girl's Girl

- **Emotional Support**: Strong female friendships give you someone you can trust when facing a difficult time. Talking to your parents or trusted adults is terrific and necessary sometimes. But having someone your age you can talk to about the big and little stuff supports your mental health and emotional well-being. You're likely to feel less lonely if you have trusted female friends, and talking things out can decrease feelings of anxiety, depression, and stress.[25]

- **Empowerment:** "Girl power" is a phrase for a reason! When girls and women stick together, they feel more powerful and supported. Women often refer to their closest friends as sisters, and "sisterhood" applies to a group of women dedicated to a joint cause. Females have the power to build each other up and support one another in a way a male friend can't.

- **Health Benefits:** Talking things over with friends, laughing, and smiling can help lower stress levels, making you feel better almost instantly. Positive, healthy friendships can boost your energy, lift your mood, and give you the confidence to take on new challenges — because you know you've got people in your corner.

- **Advocacy:** There is strength in numbers. Strong female friendships are about support and connection, not competition. When you're not competing against other girls, you can stand together to build each other up and become stronger. Through female friendships, you create a support system to reach out to when in need, and other girls will have your back in difficult situations!

- **Professional Advancement:** You're probably not worried about your future career and climbing the professional ladder — or maybe you are! However, studies have repeatedly shown that women with strong and supportive female relationships and connections have better jobs, are paid better, and have a better overall quality of professional life.

There are so many amazing benefits to female friendships! But as teenagers, it's normal for friendships and relationships to shift. Drama, misunderstandings, and changing social circles are all part of growing up and figuring out who you are — and what values matter most to you.

If you want healthy, supportive friendships, the key is learning how to stop the drama before it starts.

Spotting and Stopping Girl Drama

Girls, especially teenage girls, have a reputation for "drama." Culturally, females tend to wear their emotions more openly than males and tend to respond to situations (positive and negative) with outward displays of emotion.

Emotions are a good thing, but like everything else in life, being able to control and express them appropriately and healthily is vital. Displaying appropriate emotional control and expression is another way to be a leader! So what can you do to spot and stop girl drama in your life and build positive female relationships?

Tips to Spot and Stop Drama

- **Squash Rumors:** If you hear a rumor about someone else, even someone you don't like, refuse to participate in the drama. Don't spread rumors. And if you hear something that you *know* is false, squash it. If you wouldn't want it said about you, don't say it about someone else.

- **Practice Positive Communication Skills:** Misunderstandings happen. People say things they don't mean, or comments are taken out of context. Stay calm when communicating with others in tense or potentially dramatic situations. Practice active listening and use "I feel" statements to express your side of things.

- **Be Low-Drama:** Avoid engaging in drama and interacting with others who seem to enjoy or frequently engage in drama. Be chill and relaxed in your interactions with others in person and online.

- **Practice Empathy.** Sometimes, drama comes from not understanding the other person's point of view. Do your best to view the situation from their point of view. Empathy doesn't mean you need to forgive people who've hurt you or befriend people who are causing drama, but it can help lessen our dramatic feelings and reactions.

- **Learn to Apologize and Make Amends:** When you've made a mistake, spread a rumor, participated in unnecessary drama, etc., be the one to apologize and, if possible, make amends. We can't fix all the problems we cause, but if it is possible to do something to help or be a part of the solution, make the offer.

- **Know When to Tell an Adult:** Sometimes, the drama goes beyond what is OK or healthy. If you know someone is being bullied or threatened online or in person, it is time to get an adult involved. Likewise, if someone mentions harming themselves or others, take them seriously, even if they've said it before.

> **REMEMBER!** Strong women support other strong women. When girls join forces with one another, their self-esteem soars, and they accomplish so much more! Female friendships are important for their mental and physical health, and kindness is always a better choice than drama!

Build Up Challenge

You've heard of kindness challenges, where you have to do "X" amount of kind things to earn a reward. They're popular in elementary schools and preschools. Because you're a teen, you're getting a "Build-Up" Challenge. Your goal is to find three different ways to build up another girl today! Below are some suggestions, but feel free to create your own!

Build-Up Challenge Ideas

Compliment Another Girl On

* Her athletic performance
* Her appearance
* Her musical or dramatic performance
* A class presentation or project
* An achievement
* Something you like about her character or personality

Ask

* Another girl for help in an area you could use improvement, citing her skill in the area
* Another girl for advice, telling them why you trust them
* Another girl what her dream is and then say something supportive about it

Send/Post

* An email to a friend telling them why they're awesome
* A social media post about something one of your friends did recently that made you proud
* A handwritten note or letter to a girl you know mentioning anything positive about them

Help

* A girl in your class who is struggling with an assignment or needs a study buddy
* A woman's shelter in your community by donating feminine products like pads, tampons, deodorant, or body wash

Thank

* Another girl for helping you or inspiring you

CONCLUSION: YOUR CONFIDENCE JOURNEY STARTS NOW

> *"You are enough just as you are."*
> ~ **Meghan (Markle) Sussex, Duchess of Sussex**

You have always been enough. You were enough before you ever opened this book.

The only difference now is that you have the confidence to know it — and the tools to help you believe it every day.

This book was created to help tweens and young women like you build the tools needed to maintain daily confidence. The stories and advice inside can't give you confidence on their own — but they can guide you on your journey to finding and creating it for yourself.

Come back to the tips, activities, and stories here as often as you need. And consider sharing this book with a friend — so you can support each other and grow stronger together.

There's no one-size-fits-all path to building confidence. But if you stay patient with yourself and refuse to give up, that self-confidence will slowly become your new normal.

Think back:

- Whose story inspired you the most?
- Why did it stick with you?
- What lessons or experiences can you take from their journey and apply to your own?

Remember, real self-confidence always comes from within. But knowing that other women and girls have gone before you — facing similar fears, doubts, and challenges — and still came out on top? That can be just the spark you need to face your next hurdle with strength.

So go ahead:

- **Find your mantra.**
- **Build yourself up.**
- **Practice courage.**
- **Banish doubt.**

And most of all — **believe in you**.

You've got this.

SOURCES

1. Mark Stibich, PhD, "10 Big Benefits of Smiling," *Very Well Mind* (November 12, 2024), https://www.verywellmind.com/top-reasons-to-smile-every-day-2223755

2. Erin McDowell. "12 Athletes Who've Spoken About Mental Health Struggles," *Business Insider* (June 2021), https://www.businessinsider.com/athletes-mental-health-struggles-depression-2021-6.

3. "Self-talk," *healthdirect* (March 2024), https://www.healthdirect.gov.au/self-talk.

4. Helena Vall-Roqué, Ana Andrés, Carmina Saldaña, "The impact of COVID-19 lockdown on social network sites use, body image disturbances and self-esteem among adolescent and young women," *National Library of Medicine* (March 2, 2021), https://pmc.ncbi.nlm.nih.gov/articles/PMC8569938/.

5. Vera Feuer, MD, "Low self-esteem is a crisis among young girls. Here's how to help them," *Northwell Health*, https://www.northwell.edu/katz-institute-for-womens-health/articles/girls-self-esteem.

6. "How Teens Can Practice Reframing Negative Thoughts," *Newport Academy* (December 1, 2021), https://www.newportacademy.com/resources/mental-health/reframing-negative-thoughts/.

7. "Self-talk," *healthdirect*, https://www.healthdirect.gov.au/self-talk.

8. "5 Power Poses to Kickstart Your Confidence," *Poised and Professional* (February 2019), https://poisedandprofessional.com/2019/02/5-power-poses-to-kickstart-your-confidence/.

9. "5 Power Poses to Kickstart Your Confidence," *Poised and Professional* (February 2019), https://poisedandprofessional.com/2019/02/5-power-poses-to-kickstart-your-confidence/.

10. "U.S. teens average time spent on social networks per day 2023," *Statista Research Department* (Apr 7, 2025), https://www.statista.com/statistics/1451257/us-teens-hours-spent-social-networks-per-day.

11. "How to Finally Stop Doomscrolling," *Cleveland Clinic* (May 6, 2024), https://health.clevelandclinic.org/everything-you-need-to-know-about-doomscrolling-and-how-to-avoid-it.

12. "U.S. teens average time spent on social networks per day 2023," *Statista Research Department* (Apr 7, 2025), https://www.statista.com/statistics/1451257/us-teens-hours-spent-social-networks-per-day/.

13. Natalia Ningthoujam, "Self-reflection is the key to personal growth: Here's how to practise it," *Healthshots* (January 13, 2024), https://www.healthshots.com/mind/happiness-hacks/self-reflection-benefits/.

14. Eva M. Krockow PhD, "How Many Decisions Do We Make Each Day?" *Psychology Today* (September 27, 2018), https://www.psychologytoday.com/us/blog/stretching-theory/201809/how-many-decisions-do-we-make-each-day.

15. Jason Flack, "Public Speaking Fear Statistics: Unveiling the Numbers," *Greater Collinwood*, https://greatercollinwood.org/public-speaking-fear-statistics/.

16. Elizabeth Earnshaw, LMFT, "6 Types Of Boundaries You Deserve To Have (And How To Maintain Them)," *mindbodygreen* (December 13, 2022), https://www.mindbodygreen.com/articles/six-types-of-boundaries-and-what-healthy-boundaries-look-like-for-each.

17. "The Importance Of Setting Boundaries For Your Mental Health & Safety," *betterhelp* (February 27, 2025), https://www.betterhelp.com/advice/general/the-importance-of-setting-boundaries-10-benefits-for-you-and-your-relationships/.

18. Noam Shpancer PhD, "Feminine Foes: New Science Explores Female Competition," *Psychology Today* (January 26, 2014), https://www.psychologytoday.com/us/blog/insight-therapy/201401/feminine-foes-new-science-explores-female-competition.

19. "Our definition of bullying," *Anti-Bullying Alliance*, https://anti-bullyingalliance.org.uk/tools-information/all-about-bullying/understanding-bullying/definition.

20. Regan A. R. Gurung PhD, "Power of People: Why Being in a Crowd Feels Good," *Psychology Today* (June 15, 2021), https://www.psychologytoday.com/us/blog/the-psychological-pundit/202106/power-of-people-why-being-in-a-crowd-feels-good.

21. "What Is Mob Mentality?" *WebMD* (February 25, 2024), https://www.webmd.com/mental-health/what-is-a-mob-mentality.

22. Melanie Greenberg PhD, "The 30 Most Common Reasons People Might Criticize You," *Psychology Today* (August 26, 2014), https://www.psychologytoday.com/us/blog/the-mindful-self-express/201408/the-30-most-common-reasons-people-might-criticize-you.

23. Akihiko Masuda, Michael P. Twohig, Analia R. Stormo, Amanda B. Feinstein, Ying-Yi Chou, Johanna W. Wendell, "The effects of cognitive defusion and thought distraction on emotional discomfort and believability of negative self-referential thoughts," Science Direct (March 2010), https://www.sciencedirect.com/science/article/abs/pii/S0005791609000536.

24. Danielle Page, "The Lifelong Benefits of Strong Female Friendships," *The Well by Northwell*, https://thewell.northwell.edu/womens-health/importance-of-female-friendships.

25. Laura Barcella, "According to Science, Your Girl Squad Can Help You Release More Oxytocin," *healthline* (April 19, 2019), https://www.healthline.com/health/womens-health/benefits-of-a-girlsquad-and-female-friendships

THANKS
FOR READING MY
BOOK!

I appreciate you picking this guide to help your tween girl understand and navigate the exciting yet sometimes puzzling journey of puberty.

I would be so grateful if you could take a moment to leave an honest review or a star rating on Amazon.
(A star rating is just a couple of clicks away.)

By leaving a review, you'll help other parents discover this valuable resource for their own children. Thank you!

To leave a review & help spread the word

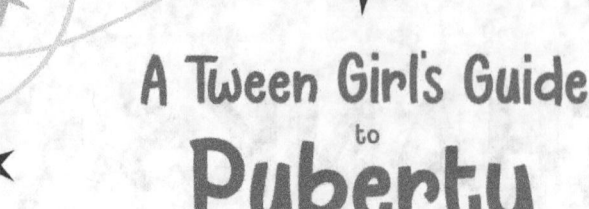

A Tween Girl's Guide to Puberty

The Complete Body and Mind Handbook for Young Girls

If you enjoyed this book, I think you'll love the first book in the series: "**A Tween Girl's Guide to Puberty.**"

Filled with practical tips, relatable examples, and simple illustrations, this guide empowers young girls with the knowledge they need to confidently embrace and savor their unique journeys.

AVAILABLE NOW ON...

amazon

Scan the code to buy a copy on Amazon

www.ingramcontent.com/pod-product-compliance
Lightning Source LLC
Chambersburg PA
CBHW071204070526
44584CB00019B/2911